Raising Lions

JOE NEWMAN

Cover design by Thomas Kepler and Sabah Quadir
Back cover photo by Martin Cohen

ISBN: 1453639683
ISBN-13: 9781453639689
Library of Congress Control Number: 2010909045

To my mother
Arlene Newman
1939 – 2009

Acknowledgements

I first want to thank my wife Julie and my stepdaughter Joan without whose constant support this book would not be possible. I want to thank my friend and editor Jane Jerrard who donated her invaluable time to this project. And a special thanks to Elizabeth Boettcher for all her assistance.

What follows are the people whose support and encouragement all contributed to my being able to complete this book: Ira Newman, Kathy Gibson, Rebecca Gradinger, Howard Sanders, Greg Tillman, Randy Olson, Ansel, Jeremiah, Francziska, Dwight, Temi, Michelle and all the staff at the Kayne-Eras/Exceptional Children's Foundation School.

I also owe a dept of gratitude to my friends in the SGI and particularly to Daisaku Ikeda for his constant encouragement.

**For updates to this book, video tutorials and
a schedule of Joe Newman's appearances
go to RaisingLions.com**

Contents

Introduction

I stood at the window of the isolation room, attempting a look of disinterest. On the other side, eight-year-old Madison screeched at the top of her voice and banged her fists violently against the Plexiglas. She'd been screaming threats, insults and demands while banging her fists against the window on and off for forty-five minutes.

Earlier that morning Madison had thrown her desk over and run out the side door of the class and through the parking lot. She'd become enraged when her teacher told her she needed to put her chapter book away and begin math. Fortunately, all the gates were closed so she didn't make it out into traffic this time, but it still took four staff ten minutes to find her hiding under a car, and another ten minutes to pull her out and carry her screaming into the isolation room. I made a note to talk to Madison's classroom staff about where they sat so they could catch her before she could make it to an exit.

Watching all this, it was hard to remember that this was the same little girl who just two days ago had stood on stage in her new blue and white dress with ribbons holding her hair in pigtails, smiling at having just won the elementary school spelling bee.

Two weeks earlier the school administrators had asked me to come in and observe Madison and tell them if I thought there was any way to turn her around. I'd done some workshops at their school and had earned a reputation for successfully transforming the most difficult children, and the administrators wanted to exhaust every option before they lost Madison to a full-time residential placement.

Raising Lions

BEHAVIOR PROBLEM CHILD

Forty years earlier, *I* was the behavior problem. As a toddler I was the kid who repeatedly stuck his fingers in the electric sockets. My mother tells of my father slapping my hand for doing this and with tears streaming down my face I looked him in the eye and did it again, then another hand slap, then again, and another slap, over and over until my father gave up and carried me away. By age three I'd learned how to use the screwdriver and began taking everything in the house apart (like the reclining chair I removed all the screws from, then watched from the closet to see what would happen – it collapsed into pieces when our neighbor sat in it.) I was aggressive with other children, knocking them over and taking their toys. When my mother brought me to the playground the other mothers would gather their children and leave.

By first grade I was getting into fights every day at school. And in the second grade they diagnosed me as A.D.H.D. and put me on Ritalin. Although the Ritalin made me a bit easier to manage, I still spent a lot of time in the principal's office. I made explosives out of model rocket engines in the basement and tested everything to see how well it would burn or what it looked like when I blew it up.

I was unfocused in school and found it difficult to sit down to read or write for more than a few minutes. My teachers described me as "not working up to my potential," or "a good student if he would just try." When you're a child who can't focus or control his impulses, most teachers treat you as if you either don't understand what's expected of you, or you simply don't care. You spend your school years annoying and/or disappointing everyone and most teachers' feeling for you is one of either condescension or chagrin.

I don't know if I would have graduated high school at all if it hadn't been for my success on the wrestling team and the fact that my mother was willing to take my dictation. Once a month she would type my papers for me while I'd pace between the kitchen and the living room calling them out to her.

Although school often left me feeling humiliated and angry, I made it through and was even admitted to the state university. (At the time they would admit you based solely on a decent SAT score.) But university looked like more of the same. Sit still, be quiet and regurgitate what we say. The only thing it seemed to offer was an education in competitive drinking, and since I'd already mastered that in high school, I didn't see the point in staying. So after seven weeks at college I shaved my hair into a Mohawk, dropped out, and went surfing.

Fortunately, I found the world was a lot nicer to me than school had been. Out in the world there was no homework. Work was engaging because it required me to learn hands-on and problem solve. I was required to come up with my own solutions to problems rather than memorize the solutions someone else came up with years ago. Learning was in context. You always knew why you needed to know something. Problems or situations at work brought up questions and then you looked for the answers. At school I could never focus on all those answers to questions I'd never asked.

During the next ten years I traveled and surfed, built furniture, became a personal trainer, and started and ran several small businesses. I'd begun to work the chip off my shoulder I'd left school with. I realized I wasn't lazy or stupid, but rather conscientious, thoughtful and smart.

At twenty-eight, although much about me had changed, I was still a party animal. And then one morning I woke up on the side of the road with no idea how I got there. Death had narrowly missed me and something inside me was deeply shaken. I started reflecting on my life so far and the inside of me cried out for a reason for my being here. During the next week the pieces of my life floated in my mind. A pattern began to emerge and things started to fit together.

I still carried the shame of being A.D.H.D. It had been a secret no one but me, the doctors and my parents knew. Ritalin was the disguise I needed to survive behind enemy lines. Every time I took that pill, I also swallowed the belief that I was broken, disordered and not like everyone else. But the last ten years had begun to teach me something else.

Instead of being the one who couldn't sit still, I was the one who kept moving and got a lot done. Instead of being unable to focus on one thing, I was able to do several things at once and adapt quickly. Instead of being too impulsive and aggressive, I was spontaneous and driven. Instead of asking too many questions, I was a good problem solver. Instead of being unable to follow the rules, I was creative and unafraid to take risks. The flip side of those characteristics that had been called a disorder, and needed fixing with medication, were actually my strengths. It had taken twenty-eight years to realize, but I was a lion.

The moment I put it all together, I also realized there must be millions of lions in schools across America that no one knew what to do with. And I knew I needed to find these children and help raise them.

The next day I walked into the local elementary school and said, "I'd like to work with the most difficult kids you've got, the kids who drive your teachers crazy, the ones no one knows what to do with."

CRISIS JOE

Not surprisingly, it turned out I had a knack for working with difficult kids, and seven months after I'd walked into that school I was working as the crisis intervention specialist at a camp for 280 of the country's all-star behavior problems. Since I didn't have a college degree, I'd simply applied to be a counselor. But after I told the owner of the camp my background and my realization about A.D.H.D. being more a gift than a disorder, he asked me to be one of two crisis intervention specialists. The other crisis intervention specialist had a Ph.D. and would train me on the job.

That summer at camp was exhilarating. I'd be working with a particularly difficult bunk when the P.A. system would announce, "Crisis Joe to G15, Crisis Joe to G15," and I'd run up to bunk G15 to find a nine year-old girl with a broomstick, two broken windows and her counselor backed into a corner trying to fend off the blows.

I had good instincts, and the kids I worked with turned around. Perhaps because I'd been so much like them, I knew what needed to be done in critical moments. I didn't take it personally when kids threw tantrums or tried to manipulate me, because I intuitively understood why they were doing it. Because I had struggled to harness the same unruly mind each of these children had, I brought to my work a vision of the capacity they had for self-control and what needed to happen to bring that self-control to the surface. When I saw a child who was inappropriate or manipulative, I could usually sense that this was coming from the child's acute sense of social dynamics, *not a lack of capacity* to understand social dynamics, as most people assumed.

When I told people about the work I did, they'd say, "You must be so patient." But I wasn't patient. I was just thoroughly engaged.

During the next eight years I worked in every capacity I could with difficult children. I was able to parlay my success rate with very difficult children to land all kinds of different jobs. I worked as a teacher, a teacher's aide, a behavior specialist in public and non-public schools; I helped found a charter school; I founded a mentoring program; and I designed an education program for the summer camp were I was initially the crisis interventionist. I worked with children between the ages of two and eighteen; children who'd been diagnosed as A.D.D./A.D.H.D, bipolar, emotionally disturbed, oppositional defiant and autistic spectrum, as well as children who were undiagnosed but simply had wild and difficult-to-control behaviors.

BACK TO SCHOOL

After eight years of working with children I realized that I needed to confront the last of the demons that still haunted me from my grade school years. I knew I needed to go back to school myself. For too long the anger that fueled my work had also stood in the way of my completing my education. I had resisted it for as long as possible.

I went back to school and completed a bachelor's and a master's degree at Antioch University in Los Angeles. When it came time to decide what to study for my master's degree, I knew I didn't want to go the traditional route (i.e. education or psychology). The last thing I wanted to do was spend two years studying how to recognize various disorders in the children I worked with; this was the paradigm I had always been surrounded by—and the paradigm I thought was flawed. Time and time again I would work with a child whom a professional educator or psychologist had labeled as emotionally disturbed, bipolar, autistic spectrum or oppositional defiant, only to find that I could transform many or all of their difficult behaviors within a single year. These labels of disorder seemed so fatal that they severely limited the vision and expectations of those who worked with them.

I decided to study organizational management, a program where I could learn communication dynamics, conflict resolution, motivation and systems of interaction. Organizational management studies group psychology as it applies to adults in work environments, and the field is driven by the business bottom line. In other words, if the theory works and people are happier and perform better, only then is the theory considered valid. In the business community, when an employee or group of employees isn't performing, diagnosing and medicating them is not an option. Consequently, businesses spend a lot of time examining how systems of interaction influence behavior, performance and motivation.

THE MEDICAL MODEL

Modern psychiatry views children like Madison, those with inappropriate or difficult behaviors, as children whose brain chemistry/ neurology is dysfunctional. Psychiatrists gather information about the specific kinds of problem behavior so they can find out what kind of disorder might account for the child's behavior. The disorder manifests as a chemical difference in the brain that causes the child to act different than other children. Sometimes, but not usually, this chemical difference can be measured, thereby confirming the diagnosis. Finally, medication is prescribed to correct or counter the abhorrent brain chemistry.

In brief, psychiatry views bad behavior as caused by bad brain chemistry. Make a diagnosis (a theory about what kind of chemical dysfunction is present), then prescribe chemicals to correct or counter the effects of the bad chemistry. Bad chemistry plus corrective chemistry equals good chemistry and good behavior.

This seems reasonable enough—until you consider that, _while brain chemistry causes behavior, it is also the case that behavior causes brain chemistry_. We know that if we send a soldier to the war zone in Iraq for a year, that when he comes back he may have post-traumatic stress disorder (PTSD). Exposure to a set of behaviors and experiences altered his brain chemistry. If this can happen to an adult's brain, how much more sensitive to behaviors and experiences is the very malleable brain of a child?

7

In other words, if a child develops a pattern of behavior or is in a system of behavior interactions that are dysfunctional, then brain chemistry can shift to dysfunctional. And if this is the case, then a child whose brain chemistry is dysfunctional can shift back to functional when she is exposed to corrective behavior interactions.

What I was doing when I was turning around these various children was creating behavior interactions and patterns that countered and remedied the interactions and patterns that had caused the bad behavior and chemistry. And in so doing, I was creating new experiences that altered not only behavior but corrected brain chemistry. The thrust of this book will show how to create new and well-thought-out methods of interactions that can alter brain chemistry, behavior and child development for the better without any medications.

The methods and approaches I've developed are not designed to simply *manage* children with difficult and dysfunctional behaviors; rather, they are designed to change the root causes of the behavior and thereby change the child's internal processes, neurology and brain chemistry.

In a July 2008 article in *The Atlantic Monthly,* Nicholas Carr wrote,

> The human brain is almost infinitely malleable. People used to think that our mental meshwork, the dense connections formed among the 100 billion or so neurons inside our skulls, was largely fixed by the time we reached adulthood. But brain researchers have discovered that that's not the case. James Olds, a professor of neuroscience who directs the Krasnow Institute for Advanced Study at George Mason University, says that even the adult mind 'is very plastic.' Nerve cells routinely break old connections and form new ones. 'The brain,' according to Olds, 'has the ability to reprogram itself on the fly, altering the way it functions.'

Introduction

OUR CONNECTIONS TO OUR CHILDREN

I've always felt that most problem behaviors in children can be remedied by shifting the ways the adults around them act. In other words, if you want to understand why a child is misbehaving, study the behavior of the adults.

It seems crazy to me that we spend so much effort trying pinpoint the source of problem behavior within the individual child, and spend so little effort trying to understand children's behaviors as shaped by their interactions with adults. Mine is a systems approach; I look at the details and the implications of the interactions between adults and children. Children's behaviors cannot be looked at in isolation.

When I watch a child I'm never thinking, "What is the neurological disorder that would cause this behavior?" Instead I always ask myself, "What's the motivation for that child's behaviors?" And, "What pattern of interactions might have created these behaviors?" And, "How are the adults around that child behaving and are those behaviors reinforcing the problem behaviors?" And finally, "What kinds of responses, language and environmental conditions are needed to change this dysfunctional system and create a system of interaction that will develop and strengthen healthy behavior and psychology?"

From the beginning of my work with behavior problem children, my experience showed me that inappropriate behaviors in children were more the result of external and controllable factors than they were the result of internal and uncontrollable factors. Ironically, the perspective in this country is that the primary, perhaps only, important factor is DNA. Most behavior problems are seen as a consequence of a disorder, a neurological problem or some other predetermined characteristic. So the solutions that are emphasized are pharmaceutical. Since my experience has shown me that most of what shapes a child's behavior is controllable and entails changing the things *outside* the child, it was a simple decision for me to focus all my attention on finding ways to change behavior that focus on the neglected two-thirds of the equation: environment and interaction.

WHAT THIS BOOK IS ABOUT

This book will explain why today's children are more willful, more difficult to raise and more psychologically feeble than children thirty years ago. Then I will show you how to change the way we raise these children to assure they become stronger, healthier and happier. I will show how to prevent and turn around relatively minor problems as well as the more severe problems like those of Madison.

This book will show how the only difference between a child who is simply strong-willed and a child who is diagnosed as disordered is a few more steps down the same path. Most "disordered" children are simply strong-willed or precocious children whose behaviors have escalated based on patterns of interaction that can be understood and reversed.

There are many books available that in effect say, "Here are effective tools and methods to use with your strong-willed child", or "Here's how to best manage and deal with a child who has a psychological/behavior disorder." What I'm saying is, "If you raise your strong-willed child using the methods in this book, he won't develop a psychological/behavior disorder or become psychologically feeble. And if he's already developed a behavior disorder here is what happened and this is what you need to know to bring him permanently back to mental health."

While diet, genetics, television and video games certainly play their roles influencing our children's behavior and development, they do not play the central role. For the last eighteen years I've watched one child after another change; children who'd been diagnosed as disordered, who'd been thrown out of school, who'd been medicated, who'd been labeled and written off. These children came back because I changed the way we interacted with them.

The way we interact with our children is the single most important factor that will determine their behavior and their mental health. We are responsible for the exponential growth in psychological disorders in our children. Our children are fine. It's us who have to change.

WHO THIS BOOK IS FOR

I wrote this book for everyone who has children or who works with children. This book will show parents, teachers and professionals more effective ways to raise, manage and motivate our children without resorting to powerful psychiatric medications. It will show parents and teachers how to raise children who are psychologically healthier, have stronger self-discipline and are better prepared to succeed in life, school, work, community and relationships.

This book will show you how a shift has occurred in the development of children as a result of changes in how we raise them. The effect of this shift varies from mild to severe. How the shift affects the individual child depends on the innate characteristics of the child combined with the extent to which they are exposed to the shift. Consequently, there has been an exponential increase in the number of children with behavior problems and psychological disorders. This shift can be reversed. The children who are psychological casualties of this shift can be rescued. I know, because I've come to understand what is causing the shift, and I've been rescuing these children successfully for eighteen years.

MADISON

When I first began my work with Madison she had been at the private special needs school for two years. Despite her being given powerful mood stabilizers like Lithium and Depakote and having a four-to-one student to teacher ratio at the school, Madison had only gotten worse. She'd been variously diagnosed as oppositional defiant, bipolar disorder and emotionally disturbed. The psychiatric medications had limited, inconsistent results. Her rages were becoming more and more frequent. She would throw textbooks across the room, constantly argue with and manipulate others, run away from class and when staff tried to stop her she would thrash, kick and scream. She would commonly throw over several desks and tear papers and posters off the walls before the staff could contain her.

By the time I'd been called in, Madison's tantrums had become so violent and regular that she needed to be carried to the isolation room three to five times a day. Her therapists and teachers were at a loss as to what to try next.

I designed an intervention using the methods and tools in this book and got everyone she interacted with at school on the same page. They each used the same language during conflict. They consistently used the exact same positive and negative consequences. They coordinated their actions so each person's effort was synchronized with and supported by the others.

Nine months after we began the intervention, Madison was back in a regular school without medication or a behavior aide. Almost three years later she is an A student at her local public school free from medication or behavior problems.

Chapter 1

The Anatomy of a Lion

Today's parents and teachers are creating lions. Current approaches to parenting and teaching develop children who are strong-willed, confident, self-assured and unafraid to speak their minds. But while we are creating lions, we are behaving like lambs. Our child rearing has become overprotective, indulgent, deferential and hypersensitive. The problem is, lambs cannot effectively raise lions.

Lions are either born or made. When children are empowered, deferred to and praised early in life they become lions. Some children are born lions, naturally strong-willed and competitive, and are then made even more powerful through child-rearing methods that empower them and make them the center of everything.

Let's be clear: I like lions. I think raising children who are lions is a good thing, provided you're ready to parent like lions. But we've tried to empower our children by giving them all the power. We are raising lions because we want our children to be powerful people, but powerful people need powerful boundaries. When children feel powerful but lack the self-discipline and self-control that comes from firm boundaries, their psychological well-being is thrown out of balance.

Consequently, the psychological health of our children is rapidly declining. In the last twenty years there has been a quadrupling of children who are taking psychiatric medications. In the last ten years there has been a 4000% increase in the number of children diagnosed with bipolar disorder, a 400% increase in prescriptions written annually for stimulant drugs to increase attention and a 333% increase in the use of antidepressant medications for children.[1,2] Children are more willful and difficult to handle. Virtually all parents will tell you that the "terrible twos" should now be called the "terrible threes, fours and fives."

I have come to the realization that the sharp rise in behavior problems and psychiatric illness in our children can be understood as the consequence of a shift that has occurred in a crucial stage of their psychological development. This shift is a result of the fundamental change in how we raise children. Not every child has been affected in the same way by this shift and its effects vary from mild to severe. How the shift affects the individual child depends on the innate characteristics of the child combined with the extent to which they are exposed to the shift.

OUR CHILDREN ARE NOT ISLANDS

Our children's behavior, intellect and emotions are deeply connected to us through the web of our interactions.

In order to talk about the current problems we face in child rearing, in the next couple of pages I will lay out a basic framework in which to understand children's psychological development. This developmental theory is intersubjective.[3] By intersubjective I mean that this theory looks at child development with a focus on the interactions between subjects (the child and mother, father, teacher, etc.). This isn't to say that children are entirely shaped by their interactions. Anyone with children knows that two children raised almost exactly the same way can turn out completely different. Rather, it is the interactions between the particular nature of the child and their relationships and experiences that will determine the development of the child.

The Anatomy of a Lion

POWER AND CONNECTION

There are two abilities that are essential to healthy child development and psychological health throughout a lifetime: *power* and *connection*.[4] Psychological health requires that a person develop a balance of both these abilities.

Power is recognition of self. When 16-month-old Emily climbs onto the big chair for the first time and says, "Look Mommy!" or three-year-old Michael says, "No! Mine!" when another child tries to take a toy from him, they are exercising their power. *Power* is the ability to recognize and take initiative based on your own wants, needs, interests and opinions. Being able to ask for or take what you need, speaking your mind and feeling confident about your abilities are all examples of power.

Connection is recognition of others. When three-year-old Hannah puts her toys away because her mom says it's time to clean up or when four-year-old Andrew refrains from pushing or grabbing and instead tells the teacher when a two-year-old at preschool takes the blocks he was using, they are exercising connection. *Connection* is the ability to connect with others. Respecting the needs and desires of others, a capacity for close friendships, empathy for others and intimate relationships are all results of ability for connection. Self-discipline is a natural consequence of connection.

By the time I left high school my sense of my own power and worth (recognition of self) had taken a beating. The authoritarian and judgmental methods teachers used to set boundaries had left scars. After ten years spent repairing those scars, the last thing I wanted to do was create them in someone else. My challenge was to set firm boundaries (recognition of others, connection) that also acknowledged and respected the spirit and independence of the child (recognition of the child, power).

A Cultural Shift: From Connection to Power

The cultural shift in how we treat children has caused the current rise in psychological illness. One way to understand this is to look at how we as a nation have shifted in what we view as important in our child rearing.

In 1924 when sociologists asked mothers which traits they wanted their children to have they named strict obedience, loyalty to church and good manners (recognition of others, connection).[5] But as parents became more aware of the fact that many authoritarian methods of parenting (recognition of adults while negating the child) were producing adults who had very little power, more and more emphasis was placed on raising children who were empowered and had high self-esteem (recognition of self, power). This led to the current opinion that the best possible methods of parenting and teaching were "child-centered." By 1988 the traits mothers most wanted in their children had shifted to independence and tolerance.[6] Recognition of the adult has lost its importance, and recognition of the child has become the central focus of child rearing (recognition of child and negation of the adult).

Consider that a hundred years ago, most people stayed married to the same person for a lifetime because of strong ability for connection, even if they were unhappy. Today more people are self-confident and able to express their wants and needs—while unable to have relationships that last very long.

The pendulum has swung from a priority of teaching children the importance of recognition and consideration of others, to the priority being to teach them recognition and consideration of self; from an emphasis on self-discipline to an emphasis on self-expression.

The problem is, an imbalance in either direction causes unhappiness and suffering. While today's imbalance is manifesting in children who are harder to control and in a sharp rise in psychological illness among our new generation, mental illness one hundred years ago wasn't nonexistent; rather, it manifested in various psychological "issues" that damaged a person's ability to direct their life in an empowered and self-confident way. When the importance was placed on the connection and consideration of others but not on recognition of your own needs, people's suffering/illness was directed inward. Today, with the importance being placed on the recognition of self and not connection or responsibility to others, people act out their suffering in their behavior, aloud, toward others.

Of course this shift in child rearing hasn't affected every child, everywhere. Many parents and teachers use methods with their children that maintain a balance between power and connection. However, this is not the norm. Day after day for the past eighteen years I've gone into schools and homes that use child-rearing methods that aren't effective with strong-willed children, very competitive children or little alpha-males and alpha-females. When these lions are raised with a lot of power and not enough connection, their behaviors escalate until they are difficult or impossible to control. And many of them develop patterns of behavior that form the basis for a conduct or attention disorder. Fifty years ago these children would have been called precocious. Today many are being medicated for a psychological disorder.

Furthermore, child rearing that doesn't insist that children recognize adults at least as equally as adults recognize them doesn't do justice to any child. The majority of children now entering college is more narcissistic, more prone to depression and feels less connected or responsible to those around them than any other generation in the last seventy years.[7]

It is not sufficient to simply try to pull the pendulum back to somewhere in the center, where there is less power and more connection.

Rather, it is time to demonstrate new models of interaction that can raise children with both a strong sense of their own power and a strong capacity for connection with others. Let's not swing from one extreme to the other; let's move forward.

We don't need to stop teaching our children they are lions. We need to become adult lions who are capable of raising our stronger, more willful children.

PENDULUM IN MID-SWING

I was born strong-willed, competitive and difficult to control (a lion). I was not, however, made more powerful and willful from child-rearing methods that praised and empowered me. Being born in 1963 I was at the tail end of authoritarian parenting and missed the self-esteem parenting that started in the eighties. Had I been raised with the empowering parenting methods of today, I may well have been impossible to control.

That first day when I walked into the elementary school to volunteer, I walked in as someone who had just come to the realization that he was a "lion." And I wanted to work with children who were also lions, children whose lion characteristics were misunderstood, squashed and labeled as mine had been. But things had changed since I'd been at school. Children had become bolder and more willful. The number of lions had multiplied and was growing.

I recognized two dominant approaches to handling lions. First was the approach I had experienced in school: authoritarian, judgmental and punitive (negate the child and recognize the adult). The second was deferential, permissive and overly positive (recognize the child and negate the adult).

18

Quite often when I would watch teachers and parents use the second, "kid gloves" approach I would think to myself, "That kid is going to eat them alive! Hell, if they'd given me that much rope as a kid, I'd have eaten them alive." Fortunately, they hadn't given me that much rope and my behaviors never escalated to the levels of many of the children I work with today.

The way children viewed themselves in relation to adults (their self-identity) was shifting.

DEVELOPMENT OF SELF-IDENTITY IN CHILDREN

The changes in our culture, media and child rearing that shifted the importance from recognition of others (connection) to the recognition of self (power) have unwittingly caused a fundamental shift in the development of our children's self-identities. The self-identity of a child determines the rules and assumptions with which he views himself, others and the world around him, and to what extent he has developed certain emotional abilities necessary to successfully navigate life's challenges and difficulties. A child's self-identity develops through three stages: **oneness, omnipotence** and **interdependence**.[8]

The first self-identity is **<u>oneness</u>** because the child does not yet fully recognize the separation between himself and those around him.[9] This stage is from birth to around fourteen months. It is only at around fourteen months that the child realizes that his mother makes her own decisions.[10] Until this point, the mother, while a separate person, seems effortlessly guided by the child's wishes and desires. The child in oneness will fearlessly crawl off the edge of the table fully expecting to be caught before he hits the floor.

Oneness

Others are not separate from self

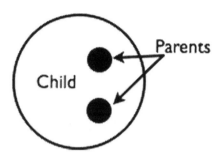

Then, at around fourteen months, the child realizes that he and his mother are independent and he is limited in his abilities and dependent on the mother for his survival. The child's previous joy and euphoria at being able to explore and exercise his power without fear vanishes with the realization that the mother could decide not to do what the child wants. (Mom *could* decide not to catch you.)[11]

At about 14 months old

Recognition of Self

Child realizes that others are independent and separate

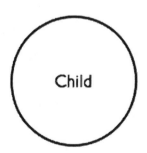

This anxiety and fear from the toddler's newly realized vulnerability drive the child to try and make his world safer by attempting to assert his will over everything. The toddler insists that the parent share everything, validate his discoveries, give in to his demands and participate in all his deeds. The child becomes a tyrant in an attempt to get the parents to give him not only everything he needs, but everything he *wants*.[12] And what he wants is complete control. Because the child has now shifted into imposing his newly discovered willpower over others, but hasn't yet discovered that others have wants, needs and willpower of their own, this second stage is called __omnipotence__.[13]

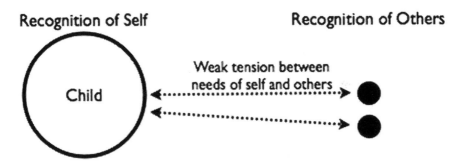

Beginning of Omnipotent Stage

Recognition of Self   Recognition of Others

Child

Weak tension between needs of self and others

The stage when the child's self-identity is **omnipotent** is a stage of conflict. Commonly referred to as the "terrible twos," it is a battle between the child's attempt to assert his will over his parents and the parents' ability to set firm limits and boundaries. (When, as a toddler, I continued to defy my father and repeatedly put my finger on the electric socket, I was exercising my power from an identity of omnipotence.) Almost all of the problems I see in the children I work with stem from issues that began during the omnipotent stage. However, if parents are successful at setting firm boundaries and strongly asserting their own will during this stage, the child will shift out of omnipotence and begin the third stage of **interdependence** at around age three.[14, 15]

Omnipotence begins to fade and self regulation strengthens

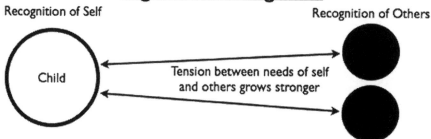

The third stage is called **interdependence** because the child realizes he is both independent of others and dependent on them. At this stage he has realized that others, like himself, have power and desires and he has developed the ability to regulate his emotions and desires in balance with, and consideration of, the emotions, needs and choices of others.

The key to a healthy transition into interdependence is to preserve in the child a sense of being recognized while bringing him fully into the recognition of others. This state is called **mutual recognition** and is the basis for healthy psychological functioning.[16]

Children should be transitioning from oneness to omnipotence at around fourteen months old and they should be transitioning from omnipotence to interdependence at around age three. There is some remnant of each identity that remains throughout the child's life. It is the strength and dominance of the different identities that determine how a child views himself and those around him, his abilities of self-regulation, his capacity for intimacy and his behavior at any given time.

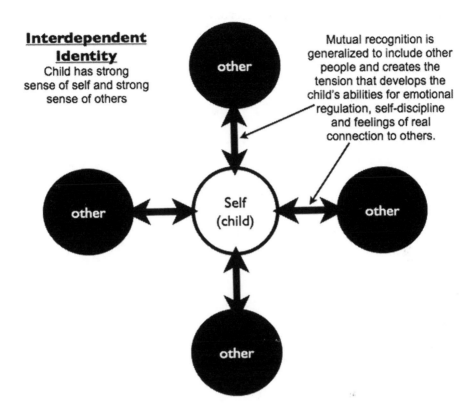

THE DEVELOPMENTAL SHIFT

Because of factors I will outline below, most of our nation's children are not transitioning to the ***interdependent*** identity as early and as completely as children did in the past. Consequently, many children's dominant self-identity remains ***omnipotent*** long past age three, and they have underdeveloped abilities for self-control, emotional regulation and recognition of others. Understanding how a child with a strong omnipotent identity sees and reacts to the world is the key to recognizing how a majority of the psychological disorders suffered by children in this country are the result of, or at a minimum are greatly exacerbated by, this developmental shift. Understanding omnipotence is also the key to creating effective strategies to healing these disorders.

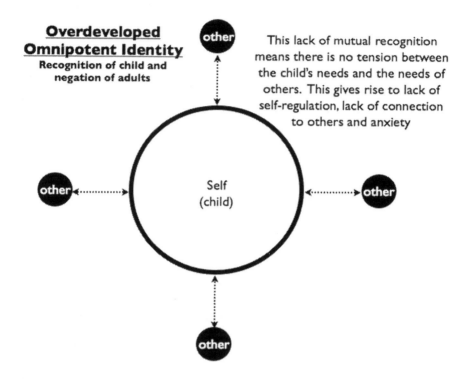

Overdeveloped Omnipotent Identity
Recognition of child and negation of adults

This lack of mutual recognition means there is no tension between the child's needs and the needs of others. This gives rise to lack of self-regulation, lack of connection to others and anxiety

other

other Self (child) other

other

OMNIPOTENCE MAGNIFIES PROBLEM BEHAVIORS

The longer a child remains in the omnipotent identity after age three, the higher the likelihood she will develop patterns of interaction and behaviors that could be diagnosed as various conduct and behavior disorders. As she develops these patterns, her sense of omnipotence is further strengthened and the behaviors become stronger and more severe. The stronger the omnipotent identity when a child enters adolescence and young adulthood, the more susceptible she is to other psychological difficulties such as depression, addiction and narcissism.

The Anatomy of a Lion

The willful characteristics of the omnipotent identity, if allowed to remain dominant into a child's third, fourth or fifth year, become strengthened by the new physical, cognitive and verbal skills the child has learned; tantrums and manipulations become more powerful, more complex and consequently much more difficult to handle. This makes it more likely that the child will succeed in getting her way, thus reinforcing her tantrums and manipulations as well as her sense of omnipotence. A child of five, six or older who has the intellectual, cognitive and language abilities of any other child her age, but internally is still functioning from the emotional self-identity of a two-year-old, will be much more difficult to handle than a two-year-old, and will exhibit behaviors and emotions that seem abnormal and disordered.

These abnormal and seemingly disordered behaviors develop in different ways depending on the characteristics of the individual child and the environments she experiences. When these behaviors are mild you get children who are simply very badly behaved, but when they are more extreme these children are diagnosed as bipolar disorder, autistic spectrum disorder, emotionally disturbed, oppositional defiant or some other neurological-based conduct disorder. By the time children have been referred to me, they have either already been diagnosed with a disorder or the parents and/or teachers are wondering if they should be.

There are two kinds of calls I typically get. The first is from an administrator or parent who is at a loss as to how to manage a child whose behaviors are continuing to escalate (i.e. Madison in the introduction). The second is from a parent who is freaking out because the teacher(s) at school have told him that they think there is something wrong with his child and perhaps she has a disorder that needs diagnosing and medicating. I received a call like this from the parents of four-year-old Ethan a few months ago.

Ethan had just turned four and was at a preschool where his behaviors had gradually been getting worse all year. His hands always seemed to be in someone's face or grabbing them. He was annoyed when he wasn't the center of attention and would disrupt the activity of the person who was. Ethan always wanted to be first in line, or in races and I watched him grab a boy by the hair who was running ahead of him and throw him to the ground so he could be first. His mother often heard other children talking about how they didn't like or want to play with Ethan.

As I watched Ethan I saw a strong-willed child who was very similar to myself at his age. Except Ethan's behaviors and aggression were being fueled by the steroids of a still dominant, and more powerful, omnipotent identity.

Ethan was still motivated by his feelings of omnipotence. His parents and the preschool staff didn't know how to set boundaries that effectively frustrated his inappropriate behaviors. So rather than coming up against boundaries that thwarted his attempts at controlling and dominating those around him, his inappropriate behaviors were successful in allowing him to get what he wanted and this further strengthened his feelings of being more powerful and important than everyone else (omnipotence).

While this may not sound like the basis for a psychological disorder, imagine the implications for a four- or five-year-old. If a child has successfully maintained control through tantrums and manipulation, or feigning inability, he will rightfully believe that he is the most powerful and capable person in the house/school. If this is true, who is in control of things? The child feels as though it is he and the unknown world he is just discovering becomes a place he must control at all costs. A sense of fear and isolation will create anxiety that drives the child to further assert his power and will. This is not a logical, but rather an emotional, decision. Children with a strong omnipotent identity will instinctively push the boundaries and try to control the adults around them until they have transitioned into a self-identity dominated by a sense of interdependence.

Imagine the omnipotent identity as the water in a river and the boundaries and interactions used by parents as the banks of that river. Increase the volume of water too much or weaken the banks and the water cannot be contained. The boundaries and interactions that assure a child transitions to the interdependent identity can be called the *system of interaction*. So the omnipotent identity is stronger, the system of interaction is weaker, the powerful omnipotent identity cannot be contained and the omnipotent identity continues to be the primary self-identity of children well into their school years.

Because of the success we've had at empowering them, most children today have "water levels" that are higher than those of children a generation ago. Some children are born with characteristics that give them water levels that are already near the top of the river's banks (naturally willful, aggressive or competitive children). For them all it takes is a bit of excess omnipotence to swell the river over its banks and start a negative cycle of behavior and self-identity.

As a result of this, many children who have average or above-average language and cognitive skills continue to exercise the self-regulation of a two-year-old. While these children's communication, physical and cognitive abilities develop as well as previous generations, emotionally they are still stuck in omnipotence. The exponential rise in behavior and emotional disorders in children, the sharp rise in adolescent depression and narcissism, and the greater difficulty parents and teachers have with unruly children can all be understood as functions of omnipotence.

Raising Lions

Understanding the problem of the omnipotent identity not only provides insight into the causes of these problems, it also provides solutions to turning these problems around and raising a generation of children who will be happier, healthier and stronger in the future. We've taken the first steps to raising lions, now it's time to raise lions who have self-control, self-discipline and a strong respect for, and connection to, others.

NOTES

1. Benedict Carey, "Bipolar Illness Soars as a Diagnosis for the Young," *The New York Times,* September 4, 2007.

2. Hara Estroff Marano, *A Nation of Wimps* (New York: Doubleday Broadway, 2008), 3.

3. Jessica Benjamin, *The Bonds of Love* (New York: Pantheon Books, 1988), 9.

4. Among intersubjective theorists such as Jessica Benjamin, what I call "power" is often referred to as "agency" or "assertion" and what I call "connection" is referred to as "recognition" or "intimacy."

5. Jean M. Twenge, *Generation Me* (New York: Free Press, 2006), 24.

6. Ibid.

7. Ibid.

8. The three stages of Oneness, Omnipotence and Interdependence is a developmental model I developed based on the insights and frameworks of intersubjective psychoanalytic theory. The model focuses on the child's perception of himself in relationship to others, particularly the mother or primary caregiver, and how this influences behavior, self-regulation, motivation and intimacy.

9. What is called "oneness" in my model is often broken into several sub-phases in other developmental models. What these other development theories generally agree on is that between 12 and 16 months of age, the child awakens to his separateness, vulnerability and dependency and enters a stage of conflict with the parent characterized by an asserting of his power and independence. This is commonly referred to as the "rapprochement crisis."

10. Benjamin, *The Bonds of Love*, 34.

11. Ibid., 34.

12. Ibid., 35.

13. The term "omnipotent" is used by Jessica Benjamin as the defining characteristic of the child in the rapprochement crisis in her *The Bonds of Love,* page 34.

14. The term "interdependence" refers to when the child has shifted into the beginnings of mutual recognition. In this identity the child has, in the words of Jessica Benjamin, begun "to come to terms with the difficulty that his own freedom depends on other's freedom, that recognition of independence must be mutual. This is a state of 'constant tension' between the needs and recognition of the self and the needs and recognition of others." (*The Bonds of Love,* 36)

15. I mark the transition into interdependence at around age three, because this is the age that child developmental theorists mark as the end of the rapprochement phase. The rapprochement phase corresponds to the omnipotent phase in my model.

16. Benjamin, *The Bonds of Love,* 16.

Chapter 2

The Lion Cub

I was recently in a client's home talking with them about their five-year-old and was able to observe the interactions between the parents and their younger son, Jacob.

Two-year-old Jacob is charming but needs constant attention. The parents are taking turns accommodating him and his needs. Jacob is curious about a dish of olives and his father puts one in his mouth; Jacob doesn't like it and spits it back into his father's hand. Now the toddler decides the olives must go. He climbs onto the coffee table and grabs the bowl of olives. The father catches the bowl before he can throw it and asks, "What do you want to do?"

The toddler ignores his father and tries to pull the bowl from his father's hand. The father says, "No thank you, we don't throw olives."

But the toddler is unfazed. "No Daddy, no Daddy," he says while he tries to pry his father's fingers off the olive bowl. During the next ten minutes the toddler keeps coming back to try and grab the olives. Sometimes he gets his hand on an olive and throws one before a parent can stop him.

They explain to him not to do it. They try to distract him with other things, but at no time do they firmly say "no" or give him any kind of consequence for ignoring their directions. I got the impression that if the father had been fast enough to catch olives thrown in every direction without letting any hit the floor he would have let his son throw them.

A few minutes later Jacob decides he wants to play the dog like a drum, banging his hands against its back. Fortunately, the dog remains good-natured and ignores the mild beating. "It's not okay to use the dog as a drum. Do you need to bang on your drum?" the father asks, then brings out a drum and gives it to him. The toddler ignores the drum. A bit later Jacob decides it's funny to pull the dog's tail. After the parents have told him several times, "No thank you. We don't pull the dog's tail," the mother tells the boy, "I want you to say you're sorry to the dog." After repeated prodding, the boy says to the dog, "You're sorry." Having the toddler apologize to the dog means about as much to the toddler as it does to the dog.

Before I leave the mother asks me if I want to watch Jacob play his piano. I stand in his playroom for over five minutes while he happily bangs on a toddler-sized piano. It is apparent that the mother feels that she, and maybe I, should stay, listen and appear fascinated by his happy banging as long as Jacob wants us to.

I share this anecdote not because it's an example of bad parenting but because it's an example of typical, some would even say exemplary, parenting. I also share it because within these interactions are the seeds of the developmental shift that feeds omnipotence.

A TODDLER'S ACTIONS ASK QUESTIONS

A two-year-old is trying to find out how much power she has and who else has power. Her actions are asking questions: "I have power, right? Do you have power? Are you like me? What happens when I do things? Can I get everything I want? Who's in charge? Who's important?"

In the example above, the toddler is learning the rules of the home and they are: "I can do anything I want. Sometimes Mom and Dad will stop me, but I can keep trying. When I do things they don't want me to do, Mom and Dad bring me new things. Mom and Dad are not like me.

They are here to serve me. When I cry they give me things to cheer me up. They're always asking me what I want and bringing me things I ask for. I control what happens and I am the most important person in the house."

Here are rules the toddler is not learning: "Don't throw olives." "Don't play the dog like a drum." "It is important to listen to Mom and Dad." "I can't have everything I want." "There are things I can do and things I can't do." "Like me, Mom and Dad also have power and things they want." "Everyone in the house is important." "Mom and Dad are in control of what happens in the house."

I felt like my clients had been trying to make an environment for their son that was like some big interactive padded room where he could do anything he wanted and remain safe. Any desires or needs the parents had seemed to come a far second to the needs and desires of their son. While this type of environment was certainly stimulating and educational, it was missing the thing most needed: *interaction with the clearly expressed will of another*. In order for a toddler to develop connection, he must come up against the will and desires of others. There must be conflict.

"The diamond cannot be polished without friction, nor man perfected without trials."—*Confucius*

Jacob's parents were raising him to be a lion (assertive, confident, powerful) but they were parenting like lambs.

WHERE DO I END AND YOU BEGIN?

When a child is two years old, he is trying to establish where you and he begin and end. He knows he has power, but doesn't know if others (primarily his parents) have power like him. When Jacob grabs the olives to throw, he's saying, "I'm independent and I have power, right?

Am I the only one who does what they want?" He is crying out for someone to oppose him so he can affirm his independence. He is trying to emerge from the womb of oneness into the identity of interdependence. By accommodating him instead of opposing him, his parents are unwittingly pushing him back into oneness.

As I watched Jacob run his parents ragged I couldn't help but admire (relate to?) his tenacity. But I also knew that Jacob is in the middle of redefining his relationship with his parents and the world. In order for him to let go of omnipotence and move into interdependence, he must come up against a will that is stronger than his own. While he needs to oppose the boundaries that are set for him so he can establish his independence, he also needs his parents to win this power struggle so his world feels safe and in control. And in order for Jacob to develop the emotional and psychological muscles that are needed for self-discipline and self-regulation, he must experience the frustrations that come with not getting what he wants.

There is a palpable sense in most American homes with toddlers that every moment should be full of pleasure, while struggles and disappointments should be avoided at all costs. But the fact is, you either accept the struggles and disappointments now or you set your children up for even greater struggles and disappointments in the future. It's like using a credit card instead of cash. Eventually, they will find out they are not the only ones with power; eventually, they will find out that everyone has wants and needs and that often the needs of others conflict with your own.

When you are raising your toddler, always pay in cash. The sooner you can coach your child through difficulties, disappointments, frustrations and consequences, the sooner she will develop the emotional muscles needed to successfully deal with life. Every time a toddler comes up against a natural boundary or frustration, look at it as an opportunity to compassionately teach her an important skill, not as something you should try to eliminate or solve for her. When you protect your child from the consequences of her behavior, you're putting the struggle on credit so she can have pleasure in the moment. Your child will need to pay for that decision in the future, with interest.

THE PARENTING CRISIS

Psychologists refer to the stage when a child is going through the difficult transition from omnipotence to interdependence as the Rapprochement Crisis. (*Rapprochement* is French for coming back together in a new way.) This period is characterized by the following pattern: the child having willful demands and/or tantrums, the parent setting limits and consequences, the child pulling away from the parent in defiance of those limits and consequences, the child calming himself and returning to the parents' embrace. Each time this pattern repeats itself, the parent-child relationship shifts, the child strengthens his abilities of self-regulation and moves from omnipotence toward interdependence.

This stage is not only a crisis for the child, it is also a crisis for the parents. During this time period a parent must also make a big shift in his or her identity.

For the first year of life the mother is everything for her child. She is protector and nurturer. She is responsible for meeting her child's every need and for removing all frustration and discomfort.

Once her child begins the rapprochement crisis, a mother must change her role as a parent. She must make the transition from being a parent who provides for all her child's needs to the parent who coaches her child to handle many frustrations and needs himself. Parents must transition from the personal identity and ego gratification of being the problem solver and provider of all things, to exercising the self-discipline and restraint that allows their child to learn to handle many frustrations and difficulties on his own and become more independent. It is difficult for a mother to watch her child struggle and there is a strong maternal desire to remove all frustration, disappointment and discomfort. But the mother must resist this desire if her child is to develop the emotional tools necessary to thrive and transition into interdependence. Additionally, the parent must not be swayed by her child's emotional rejection and scorn that occur as a natural part of the rapprochement crisis.

In her book *The Bonds of Love,* Jessica Benjamin talks about the struggle the mother has during the rapprochement crisis:

> What the mother feels during rapprochement and how she works this out will be colored by her ability to deal straightforwardly with aggression and dependence, her sense of herself as entitled to a separate existence, and her confidence in her child's ability to survive conflict, loss, and imperfection.

Today's expectations and pressures on parents don't make this parenting crisis easier. On the contrary, they make it harder. Today's mothers are supposed to give their toddlers choices and solicit their opinions about everything; provide constant stimulation, education and entertainment; make sure they are constantly showered with praise; and keep them wrapped in the latest products to assure perfect safety and health. There is so much for a parent to keep up with today that it is no wonder that parents forget their own needs and right to an independent existence. Everywhere society is pressuring the parent with the message, "Forget your own needs. If you really love your children, you should sacrifice everything for the sake of giving your child the best of everything." But remember our consumer society isn't driven by the desire for your child's psychological health; it is driven by a market that thrives when you buy more stuff.

The Lion Cub

THE TWO HANDS

When a toddler strongly asserts her will against the will of the parent, we can imagine this as a child's hand pushing forward. The purpose of the hand pushing forward is twofold. First, the hand comes forward to exercise and confirm the child's independent will and power. Second, the hand is coming forward out of an anxiety from her new sense of separateness and vulnerability. It reaches forward looking for someone else. The hand pushing forward is saying, "I'm here, I have power," and, "Is anyone else here?" Because today's toddlers are young lions, their "hand" pushes forward more often and with more ferocity.

The authoritarian response to the toddler asserting their will is to react harshly. A child tries to take a cookie after the parent has already said no more: "I said NO! How many times do I have to tell you!" Then the parent throws the cookie in the trash. An authoritarian response uses fear, punishment, shame, guilt or judgment. The hand that reached up was smacked back down by the hand of the parent. The authoritarian response tells the child, "I (the parent) am here, and only I have power." The effect of this is that the child's sense of power is damaged. Connection is established but it is dysfunctional because it simultaneously negates the child's self. The authoritarian parent becomes omnipotent in the eyes of the child, the adult has all the power, and the child has none. This parenting approach was the most common forty or more years ago.

Today the permissive approach is more common. The response of today's parent to the toddler asserting his will is to give understanding and reasoning. This often comes in the form of communicating to the child that the behavior is not okay or negotiating with the child. For instance, the child takes a cookie after the parent has said no and the parent says, "I see you really wanted another cookie. You can have it this time but the next time you want another cookie I want you to ask Mommy *before* you take it, okay?" Then the parent lets him eat the cookie.

In this case, the hand that came up was never met by the hand of the parent. Rather, the parental hand yielded and backed away from the child's reaching hand. *The child experiences permissive parenting as abandonment.* The hand backing away tells the child, "You are here, and you do have power. But no one else is here. You are alone." The effect is the child's sense of omnipotence is strengthened. The capacity for intimacy, however, is not developed because the parent has erased herself as a real other person because she has no power or will in the eyes of her child. Therefore the child is alone with his power. Ironically, even the power the child feels from the permissive interaction is only fleeting. What the child of the permissive parent craves is recognition from someone that he recognizes as equal to himself. This is something that the parent that has allowed herself to be negated can't give.

MEET THE HAND

From these examples we can see that the ideal parenting style would develop the child's capacity for both power and connection; it would set firm boundaries and limits while affirming the child's power and independence. Imagine a hand reaching up and firmly meeting the hand of the parent in the middle. Both hands pressing together, the power of the child developed in a healthy balance with a real knowledge of and connection to another.

In the case of the toddler taking a cookie after I have said no more, it might go like this: "Oh, I see you decided to take a cookie after I said no. (I take the cookie.) When you ignore what I tell you then you have to have a time out. (I walk him over to a chair) You'll need to sit quietly for two minutes and then you can get up." He starts to cry and I say, "Yeah, time outs are no fun. Tell me when you're finished crying and we'll start your time out."

You want the child to stop crying before the time out starts, because you want him to exercise self-control. If the child starts crying when the time out is given the parent will be tempted to try to calm the child by talking to or cuddling with him. But this takes away the opportunity for him to self-regulate in lieu of parent-led regulation. It also creates a positive consequence that counters the negative consequence of the time out and reinforces the behavior you want to discourage. The act of taking the cookie may have been defiant or a lack of self-control or both. In either case, you want to create a consequence and a necessity that the child exercise self-control (stop crying and sit quietly for two minutes) before activities of the day continue.

The language, "I see you decided to" and "Tell me when you're finished" are meant to affirm the child's independence and power to choose. There is no judgment or moralizing of his decision. I firmly set the boundary, while remaining in the role of compassionate coach.

This is the difference between being bad and getting punished and choosing a cause and getting the effect. You're teaching the child that, "Yes, you have power and it's okay to use it; however, some actions lead to consequences that you might not enjoy." The metaphoric hand is met firmly by the hand of the parent and the answer to the query, "I am here and I have power. Is anyone else here?" is, "Yes, you are here, and you do have power. I am also here, and I also have power."

The will of the child must come up against a will that is stronger than his own if he is to develop a healthy ability to respect and interact with others. But the strong will of the parent should affirm and not judge the independence of the child if the child is to develop a healthy sense of self.

Along with setting boundaries, this "Meet the Hand" style of parenting encourages children to offer opinions, express likes and dislikes, and argue for what they want, so long as it was done in a respectful manner. When it was not done respectfully, then the child gets a consequence.

FAITH NEEDS A NAP

I was visiting a friend who had a two-and-a-half-year-old daughter named Faith. We had spent most of the afternoon talking and listening to music with her. While we were talking we had been listening to a gospel album that was Faith's favorite. At the child's urging we had heard the album three or four times and we were ready for something different. My friend told her daughter we were putting on something else. As soon as the new album started playing, the child began to scream for her favorite. My friend attempted to convince the girl that we needed a change. She tried to tell Faith that we would listen to her favorite after we had heard something else. She tried to tell her she needed to stop screaming. All her efforts were to no avail. Faith's screaming just got louder and more persistent. After five minutes of this my friend asked if I wanted to give it a shot. "Just follow my lead," I replied.

I went up to Faith and said, "I guess Faith needs a nap." Faith yelled even louder. Taking Faith's hand I said, "It's okay, Faith. I can see you're having a tantrum and when little girls have tantrums I know that it's time for a nap."

Faith now screamed, "I don't want a nap! No nap! No nap! Mommy, no nap! My friend said, "Joe's right. I think you need a nap."

Now, while holding her hand and moving her toward the bedroom, I said, "Faith it's okay, sometimes little girls need to have a tantrum, that's okay. But, when a little girl needs to have a tantrum she also needs to have a nap."

This back and forth between Faith yelling "no nap" and me saying, "tantrum equals nap" went on several times while I moved her toward the bedroom. Then Faith yelled, "I'm not having a tantrum!" With a calm voice and a tilt of my head I said, "You're not having a tantrum? Well you're pulling my arm and you're yelling and crying so I can see you're having a tantrum."

Faith, gaining control of herself, said in a quieter voice, "I'm not having a tantrum." I said, "Are you sure you're not having a tantrum? I understand if you need to have one. It just means you'll also need a nap. And that's okay."

Faith, now even quieter, replied, "I'm not having a tantrum. No nap."

I said, "I see you're not yelling any more. So maybe you're not having a tantrum now and you don't need a nap."

Faith said in a quiet voice, "I don't need a nap." I looked at her and said, "You understand we are not going to play your music right now, so you'll need to listen to the music we choose?"

Faith said, "Yes."

Faith stayed with us, without a nap or a tantrum for the rest of the afternoon. After she was calm, we told her that as long as she was polite she could talk to us about playing her album when this one was over. About two hours later she asked politely, for the second time and we did decide to play her album again, in part because we wanted to encourage her asserting her wishes in a respectful manner.

ACTION: YOUR CHILD'S FIRST TEACHER

Lions understand action. When my friend tried reasoning with her daughter Faith she got nowhere. Reasoning is fine—so long as it is firmly tied to action. Reasoning with your child without firm action only develops their capacity for manipulation.

The above interaction with Faith builds both power and connection. Power is developed when the boundary is set using the language of cause and effect, which emphasized Faith's choices and the consequences of those choices. Additionally, her power was developed two hours after the tantrum when she expressed her wants respectfully and got a result. Connection was developed because Faith came up against the unyielding will of the adults who, while firm, were neither judgmental nor angry at her willfulness. It is only through coming up against the opposing desires and will of another that a child develops a real sense of others existing as equal to themselves. Finally, by allowing Faith to choose either a tantrum and a nap, or self-control and staying with the adults, Faith was motivated to exercise emotional regulation and develop her abilities for self-control.

The Meet the Hand approach is one that develops mutual recognition. Children aren't born understanding mutual recognition. Rather, it is up to their parents and teachers to set boundaries and coach their children through the difficult process of developing this ability.

As this book progresses, the "Meet the Hand" approach and the goal of mutual recognition will be central throughout. As children get older and for more severe behavior problems, the techniques used to meet the hand become more sophisticated, but the principles on which they're based remain the same.

Too Many Time Outs?

There's a reason why parents tell one another that it's no longer the "terrible twos" but the "terrible twos, threes, fours and fives." The rapprochement crisis lasts longer because the omnipotent identities of our children are larger, stronger and more sophisticated. It takes longer to subdue this identity and allow transition into interdependence.

The Lion Cub

I often see parents of two-, three- or four-year-olds who are doing an excellent job setting boundaries but who ask me, "Is it supposed to be this hard?" They have children who are very bright, very willful and sometimes very physical. These are children who would be a handful if raised by any generation. But combine these natural characteristics with the empowering parenting methods being used today and you get children with extremely strong and sophisticated omnipotent identities. This means these children will challenge boundaries in stronger, more tenacious and more complex ways than any generation before them. This is only natural.

Parents need to be prepared for handling more willful and sophisticated tantrums. Problems occur when parents and teachers see these more extreme tantrums as unnatural and perhaps the sign of some neurological disorder or problem.

I recently worked with the parents of a boy named Josh who had just turned three. Josh was very large for his age and was often mistaken for a five-year-old. His coordination was so advanced he was already a confident swimmer and he enjoyed racing the five- and seven-year-old neighbors in their pool.

His parents used short time outs for Josh to good effect when he became too aggressive with other children, or too wild or disobedient. This was effective, but his parents were concerned at the amount of time outs he needed and with some difficulties at preschool. Although most days Josh needed only four or five short time outs, there were some days when he needed twenty or thirty.

One day his mother stubbed her toe on the edge of the furniture and let out a "G-d damn!" within earshot of Josh. The next day, every couple of minutes Josh let out his own "G-d damn!" and every time he did his mother gave him a one-minute time out and told him those were not words he was allowed to use. She told me she gave Josh thirty time outs that day. But by the end of the day he had stopped saying it and has never used it again.

Josh had started preschool a few months before his third birthday. It was a mixed-age preschool with thirty children between three and five years old. Josh was the youngest one there. While the preschool hours were between 9 a.m. and 2 p.m., Josh usually needed to be picked up by noon. The director said that by then he was getting too "pushy" with the other children and was difficult to control. His parents were concerned and wanted my opinion.

On closer inspection I found out that the preschool Josh went to had a very different approach to setting boundaries than his parents. The preschool didn't believe in saying no to children and they also didn't use time outs. Instead, if Josh pushed another child or refused to follow directions the staff gently redirected him and explained, "We don't do that here." So if Josh pushed another child and took their toy the staff would say to him, "Josh we don't push people here. Maybe I can help you find your own toy." Then they would show him another set of toys and encourage him to choose one.

So while Josh's parents are practicing meet the hand child-rearing, the preschool was practicing "avoid the hand" child rearing.

Josh is naturally testing the boundaries and trying to find out how things work at the preschool. From his perspective, what he sees is, "When I push someone at preschool, an adult comes over and shows me new things." The teachers at the preschool don't tell him that if he pushes others he will need to go home, so he doesn't make the connection between his actions and going home. By the time his mother has responded to the call to pick him up and driven to the preschool, at least a half an hour has passed and Josh might not have been at all "pushy" during that time so telling him he has to go home for something that happened thirty minutes ago seems pointless.

The Lion Cub

The challenging of boundaries is healthy and natural and happens for several reasons. Children assert and exercise power or omnipotence because it gets them what they want, and because this is the only way they know how to connect. It is only by pushing against others, literally and metaphorically, that a child finds out where he—and others—begin and end. Children thirst for an understanding and sense of others. When they are in the middle of experiencing their own power and sense of omnipotence, what better way than to challenge the power of others? They push the hand forward because they want to meet the hand of the other. They may fight it, but it is only to feel the firm will of the other against them. During the rapprochement crisis conflict becomes the place the child learns about others. Conflict is the opportunity to establish the skills of intimacy, connection and self-regulation.

Ten months after the first consultation I received another call from Josh's parents. The director of the preschool had suggested that they have Josh evaluated for a possible behavior disorder. Josh's physical aggression with other children and his defiance of the teachers had been increasing throughout the year.

When I went into the preschool I saw that when Josh, or any of the other children, misbehaved the staff explained to them which behaviors were okay and which weren't. But they set very few actual consequences. Josh enjoyed the attention and the conversation that followed his misbehaviors.

Problems at home had also reached the boiling point. Josh had gradually become more wild and disobedient. He would refuse to take time outs and when his mother tried to enforce them he would run away, yell insults, hit her and even spit at her. After a long and detailed discussion his parents and I realized that as Josh's behaviors had gotten more difficult, the consequences they gave him had gotten weaker. Rather than giving the time outs in the method we'd discussed, now 95% of the time they simply threatened to give them.

The truth is, not all schools are a good fit for all children. If your child is a lion, like Josh, and the preschool you've chosen thinks that children just need to talk about their feelings and discuss the rules in order to behave, your child is going to eat them alive. Josh's natural aggression and strong will were too much to be contained by the warm and fuzzy approach the preschool was using. The parents of lions need to look for schools and classrooms that have clear boundaries and consequences that are enforced consistently.

Josh and his family were lucky, as it turned out the director of Josh's preschool was very open to new ideas and solutions for working with Josh. She'd seen one or two children each year whose behaviors had slowly escalated similar to how Josh's had and she was eager to learn a method to get a different result.

With the support of the preschool director, Josh's parents and I brought in a behaviorist to work with Josh at preschool for six weeks. Before the behaviorist started I taught the parents and the behaviorist a scripted behavior protocol with specific actions and language to use when Josh was misbehaving or defiant. We also met with the preschool director so she knew what to expect.

Three days after starting the behavior protocol Josh's most aggressive and defiant behaviors had stopped completely. Everyone, including me, was surprised at how quickly Josh changed. This had a lot to do with the fact that his parents had committed 100% to doing the method at home. Although during the next three or four weeks Josh continued to test boundaries, all of his physically aggressive and defiant behaviors ended. Josh was not only following directions, he was also happier and more at ease. The preschool director asked me to teach her staff to use the methods we were using with Josh, which I did.

The Lion Cub

How Many Lions Are out There?

Imagine a child, just like Josh, whose parents and preschool teachers are committed to using only the childrearing method originally used by Josh's preschool. His sense of omnipotence might remain entirely unchecked. He would experience the "reason and distract" approach not as compassion but as abandonment. His aggressive, willful and challenging behaviors would escalate in an anxiety-driven search to meet the hand that was always pulling away. As these behaviors became more extreme and out of the norm, the school staff might incorrectly assume these behaviors are a result of an inability to reason and understand. Based on this assumption they might expend more effort reasoning and talking with him about his behaviors and actually loosen the boundaries to give him more leeway because of his perceived lack of ability to understand. By the time he was four or five he might have developed more extreme tantrums and manipulations and be diagnosed with a learning or behavior disorder.

These are the lions I see every day. Normal, healthy children who, because of an unfortunate combination of challenging characteristics, a society that has strengthened their sense of omnipotence, and well-meaning teaching and parenting methods that have backfired, now exhibit behaviors that seem so far off the norm that they must be a sign of some neurologically based disorder.

Chapter 3

Feeding Candy to Lions

EMOTIONAL DIABETICS

Raising your child on a diet of praise, deference and indulgence is like feeding them candy and cake for every meal. You'll end up with emotional diabetics; children who are too feeble to digest life's basic frustrations and difficulties.

WHY AREN'T CHILDREN TRANSITIONING OUT OF OMNIPOTENCE?

There are a number of changes that have caused our children's failure to transition out of omnipotence. These changes fall into two categories: things that have weakened the boundaries and limits adults set (requiring less recognition of others) and things that have strengthened our children's feelings of omnipotence (giving more recognition of self/child). The best way for a child to make a healthy transition out of omnipotence and into interdependence is for her to feel a strong balance of recognition of self and others (mutual recognition).

TOO MANY CHOICES

One of the ways we empower our very young children today is by giving them choices. Forty years ago, parents didn't give toddlers many choices. Today's parents are encouraged to give toddlers choices about everything.

While there is a degree of empowering choices that's healthy to give a child, this is a fundamental shift from thirty or forty years ago, and it's changing the way our children view themselves. When children get used to having choices about everything, they come to expect to be given choices about everything. By the time they enter school, many children aren't ready for a teacher who doesn't ask them, but tells them what activity will come next.

There are two problems with giving toddlers too many choices. First, it makes it more difficult later on when they find themselves in situations where they will not have choices and need to support the group (at school, for instance). The second problem is that it strengthens the child's omnipotent identity, which will make it more difficult to transition into the interdependent identity. Children who are given too many choices will be more willful during the omnipotent stage and may be too willful to control.

I met a mother of four who never let her children choose what they were having for dinner, even when they went out to eat. Her reasoning was simple; she cooked dinner for six people every night and knew she couldn't offer them choices, so she didn't want them to get accustomed to choosing their dinner. Furthermore, she wanted her children to know they were part of a team and that the needs of the many outweighed the needs of one.

Giving children choices about some things is fine, but there should be many things during a child's day where they don't have a choice, or the choices are very limited.

HE'S NOT THE ONLY ONE HERE

I watched a woman who was reading to her three-year-old grandson, Ryan. Halfway through the book Ryan had chosen, he decided he wanted her to read a different book. Grandma said, "No. You chose this book and I want to finish this one." Ryan whined and started to cry, "But I want the other one!" Ryan's mother came over and said, "Come on Mom, why don't' you read him the other one?" But the older woman wouldn't budge. "He needs to learn he's not the only one around here," she stated. By asserting her desires, Ryan's grandma was insisting that he recognize her. She was instinctively trying to establish mutual recognition.

In order for Ryan to develop a healthy capacity for mutual recognition, the adults around him must be willing to have faith in his ability to survive disappointment and frustration and not let their fear of this sway them toward overindulgence. The fear implicit in Ryan's mother's impulse to give him what he wants in this situation is, "What if he doesn't develop a love of reading?" or, "What if he doesn't learn to assert his wishes?" or maybe just "I want this moment to be one of joy, not one of disappointment."

The accumulation of so many moments when adults have yielded their wishes and desires to the wishes and desires of the child result in the imbalance toward children developing power over connection. While these moments, when viewed in isolation, appear harmless enough, the cumulative affect is a child who develops a very strong omnipotent identity.

When giving your child choices, remember that you must prepare her for being successful and happy at school. If home is a place of unlimited choices and accommodations and school is a place of limited choices and few accommodations, don't be surprised when your child doesn't like school.

Tips for Parents	
INSTEAD OF THIS	**TRY THIS**
Giving choices about everything. Clothes, food, activities, schedule, etc.… "Where would you like to go to eat?" "What time do you want to go to the park?"	**Choices about some things and not others.** "Mommy and Daddy choose where we're going to eat. At the restaurant you'll have some choices about what you'll order." "We're going to the park at 1:00." "When we go to the park you must always wear pants."
Open-ended choices "What do you want to wear today?" "What do you want to order?"	**Structured choices** "Which pants would you like to wear? The red or the blue?" "You can order the macaroni, the fish, or the hot dog."
There are always choices	**Sometimes the only choice is between doing what Mommy says or getting a consequence.**
Allowing long discussion or debate about the choices and the rules "But I don't want to go home. I want to stay at the park."	**There should be times when "no discussion" is the rule.** While short discussions should sometimes be accommodated, if your child is using questioning the rule as a way to badger you into relenting, you should give a consequence that deters them from using this approach again: "I told you I wasn't going to discuss this any more, now you'll need to take a two-minute time out."
Having choices is a right	**Having choices is a privilege that can be taken away if you don't respect the rules that govern them.**

Using the options above will allow you to create a structure within which to manage your child's wants and desires. Only after the parent has created such a structure can the child begin to internalize that structure and develop the muscles needed for self-regulation and deferred gratification.

IS YOUR CHILD'S OPINION MORE IMPORTANT THAN YOURS?

The parenting practice that is closely tied to choices is regularly soliciting the child's opinion. This can range from letting him choose what clothes he'll wear to asking his preference of which restaurant to go to, to choosing what color to paint the kitchen.

Whether it's the boy who wants to continue to wear his Halloween costume to school two weeks into November or the girl who refuses to wear anything but her favorite dress even though her mother hasn't had a chance to wash it in five days, I can't count the number of times I've seen a parent dragging a tearful, puffy-eyed kindergartener into school late after a long battle over what the child will wear.

Children who are given choices about everything learn to question anything they don't prefer. This might seem fine for a tolerant parent at home, but by the time these children enter school it becomes extremely difficult to deal with their belief that their opinions are just as valuable, or more valuable, than the opinion of their teacher.

I've seen third grade math classes where children argue with the teacher about the way she's teaching arithmetic. This isn't spirited discussion aimed at clearing up a lack of understanding, but rather an insistence that their way is correct and the teacher's is not.

A veteran teacher approached me after a seminar I gave and said, "It's like you've given us permission to be adults again." As parents and teachers, we are encouraged to provide so many choices and to elicit so many opinions from our children that we are left feeling as though our opinions are less important than those of children. We are supposed to make everything fair, consider everyone's opinion, see to it that no one is inconvenienced (except us), and that everyone's needs are met, all while facilitating some great, chaotic democracy. But in the middle of all this, have we forgotten that we are the adults? *We* should decide what is good and not good for our children.

Giving children choices and soliciting their opinions can have many positive effects *only if* you are prepared to set and hold firmer, more sophisticated boundaries to balance the powerful identity your child consequently develops.

COMMUNICATION

Today's parents talk to their children more. Parents talk to children when they're in the womb, they talk to them when they're infants, they explain to them what they're doing while changing their diapers, they verbalize things they assume the child might be feeling. ("You don't like the chicken, do you?" " Oh, you like the potatoes.") Consequently children are more articulate earlier. Parents have more sophisticated discussions with their toddlers, and children are exposed to more sophisticated dialogue on TV and the Internet. Raising more articulate children is a great thing—but it requires a change in parenting.

Thirty years ago the two-and-a-half-year-old had temper tantrums with the small arsenal of words at her disposal. Today's toddler is equipped with more words and the confidence to use them. This means that tantrums are more sophisticated and harder to respond to. Consequently, adults are more likely to acquiesce to a child's demands, and each time this happens the omnipotent identity is strengthened.

The other difficulty inherent in raising more articula^ that adults are more likely to try to reason with a toddler wɪ̣ᴏ ̣ spoken. A two-and-a-half-year-old may be able to express herself and understand at the level of a four- or five-year-old, but she is still functioning emotionally and from the self-identity of the two-and-a-half-year-old. But like Faith in the previous chapter, action must come before reason.

Not only are children more articulate, but they also understand better the subtleties of communication. They understand the implications inherent in what is said. Ironically, parents and teachers are not only communicating more to children, they are also giving them more information in situations where the child actually needs less because of their heightened abilities to understand the implications of language. This sets up unbalanced and possibly dysfunctional communication dynamics.

LESS TALK, MORE ACTION

The tendency to go to great lengths to reason with toddlers has made it more difficult for them to transition to interdependence. The problem with reasoning with toddlers when they have done something that needs correcting is that toddlers primarily understand action. In the end the only thing that really matters to them is "Did I get what I want?" Also, many discussions parents have with toddlers assume a level of ethical ability that children this age simply do not have. While the parent is trying to teach the child to understand the right or wrong of something, the child is processing her experience and even the conversation in terms of "How do I get what I want?" The only way to teach toddlers right from wrong is to create consequences that assure that what is right is in their self-interest and what is wrong is not.

Children will naturally develop the powers of reason, but they develop these powers through experiencing the consequences of their actions. If the consequences of their actions are teaching the child one thing while the words of the parents are teaching them another, then the child learns that words have no integrity and therefore it is perfectly natural to use them for manipulation.

When a three-year-old hits another child and the adult asks him to say, "I'm sorry," we aren't teaching him empathy or sympathy for others. We're teaching him that if he wants to hit someone he will also need to say the words, "I'm sorry."

In order to teach a child empathy we need to demonstrate it, not lecture about it. Rather than tell your child what he should be feeling toward someone who is hurt, demonstrate empathy when he is hurt. For instance, if your child pulls a toy away from another child who then begins to cry, give your child an immediate time out and give the toy back to the other child. Then when your child is upset because he's gotten a time out, empathize with him: "I know time outs aren't any fun. I wouldn't like it either. But when you take some one else's toy away you've got to have a time out."

Additionally, adults incorrectly assume that children naturally are, or should be, moral not immoral. The fact is children are neither moral nor immoral, but rather amoral. Therefore, children often use moral language to get what they want from adults (i.e. manipulate).

The end result of all this communication instead of consequences is that the omnipotent identity of the child seldom comes up against the firm will of another. Rather, he learns that he can continue to do as he likes, even at the expense of others, so long as he uses the correct words. With each easy dialogue he has in lieu of a difficult consequence, the more sophisticated becomes the language he learns how to use to get what he wants… and the omnipotent identity remains unscathed.

Tips for Parents

INSTEAD OF:	TRY:
Asking them to apologize "Tell your sister you're sorry" "I need you to apologize to Kevin and tell him you won't hit him again."	**Give an immediate consequence.** The consequence needs to be sufficient to outweigh the gain from the problem behavior. In other words you want them to feel sorry they did the behavior, not just say it.
Telling them how they should feel "Look at your sister crying. Don't you feel sad for her?"	**Let consequences teach.** When adults try to tell children what they should feel (empathy, compassion, generosity, etc.) what they actually feel is shame and guilt because they didn't have those feelings.
Explaining to them in detail why something is wrong	**Ask them to figure it out.** After giving a consequence, ask them questions so they can see the behavior wasn't in their self-interest. "Why did you..." "Did that choice get you what you wanted?" "What could you have done to get what you'd wanted?"
Repeatedly telling your son and his friend to stop yelling while they are watching TV.	**Take the remote and turn the TV off.** Now that you have their attention tell them "The TV is turned off for the next minute. If I have to do this again it will be turned off for five minutes. Do you understand why I turned it off?"
Telling them the rules over and over. When you tell children the rules over and over again you are trying to protect them from failure, mistakes and consequences. By letting them learn from consequences you allow them how to relax and evolve through their mistakes.	**Tell them the rule once, or not at all.** After that give short consequences so they remember and learn the rules. Repeating the rules over and over is condescending and tells them the rules aren't serious. Violent or destructive acts should be met with immediate consequences. If your four-year-old daughter throws her plate, there is no need to explain why that's not OK.

Raising Lions

THE PROBLEM WITH PRAISE

Perhaps the most overt cause of overdeveloping the omnipotent identity of children is praise. For twenty-five years, the self-esteem movement has told us that lack of success and happiness in life was a result of low self-esteem and if parents and teachers showered children with praise they would have high self-esteem and would become anything they wanted. As a result, parents and teachers praised children's every minor effort and mediocre accomplishment.

I'm not advocating abandoning praise altogether; I regularly praise the children I work with. Rather, reserve it for the moments when it is earned and use it appropriately. Praise is effective when it is warranted, specific and focuses on effort rather than intelligence.

Recent studies have shown that praising a child's intelligence, as opposed to their effort, develops children that are risk avoidant, anxiety prone, adverse to exerting too much effort and underperforming. Whereas praise given for a child's *effort* motivates the child to try harder and be bolder in their efforts.[1]

Ironically, the overuse of praise as a tool to develop self-esteem has undermined its use as an honest compliment. A series of studies by psychologist Wulf-Uwe Meyer showed that, by the age of twelve, children believe that earning praise from a teacher is not a sign that you've done well, but rather a sign you lack ability and the teacher thinks you need extra encouragement.[2]

A woman told me about how the other mothers at Girl Scout camp were angry when she refused to applaud her daughter when she received a third place trophy in "Large Animal Care." She told the other mothers, "I refuse to tell my daughter she should be proud of herself for being the third best at shoveling poo!"

Bombarding a child with praise will naturally strengthen her feeling of not only being great, but possibly of being better than everyone else. Such a child will be more willful and will require firmer, more sophisticated boundary setting in order to develop a healthy recognition of others.

Tips for Parents	
INSTEAD OF:	**TRY:**
Praising broadly: "What a genius you are." "You're fantastic."	**Be specific:** "The colors and pictures you used on your project made it a pleasure to look at."
Praising characteristics: "You're so kind." "Wow, you're really smart."	**Focus on effort:** "I saw how you went out of your way to sit next to the new girl. That was very thoughtful." "I can tell you worked really hard on this. Nice effort."
Praising everything	**Choose what deserves praise:** When everything a child does is praised, your praise becomes meaningless.
Never give criticism	**Be authentic:** Don't be afraid of telling a child you think she could do better when it's clear she hasn't given her best effort.

TOO MUCH STIMULATION

Children are given too much stimulation too early. This is not something that we can turn the clock back on. While we can, and should, limit the amount of time our children spend in front of the computer and the television, we must realize that the nature of how we entertain ourselves has been irrevocably changed. Realistic special effects, quick edits that move from one image to another, hundreds of channels to choose from, and games and computers that respond to commands or shifts in mental direction instantly are all having a profound impact on the way our children's minds develop.

The result is children with shorter attention spans, a low tolerance for boredom and a precocious attitude that drives them toward more stimulation.

Parents and teachers have responded to this shift by trying to give children more of the stimulation they desire. Parents are constantly working to keep up with their children's busy schedules. And teachers are working overtime to keep lessons entertaining and engaging.

EFFECTS AMPLIFIED BY THE MEDIA

As children's feelings of omnipotence and self-importance in-creased, the media adapted to appeal to its changing audience, and in so doing reinforced the cycle of omnipotence and provided role models. Perhaps the most blatant example of the psychology of the omnipotent child was presented in the "Home Alone" movies. In "Home Alone 2" the main character, ten-year-old Kevin McAllister, is once again unwit-tingly abandoned by his parents. This time he lands in New York City and has no difficulty securing a cab, hotel and room service. At every plot turn, ten-year-old Kevin shows the highest character and wisdom while the adults are portrayed as gullible boobs with little to no charac-ter or wisdom. Not only does Kevin possess MacGyver-like skills and ingenuity, but he is also the only character in the film to show a depth of wisdom, compassion and good sense. By the middle of the film, Kevin has been elevated to the level of guru when he counsels a homeless woman to face her demons and rejoin society.

This film was successful because it reflected the inner feelings of a generation of children who believe they are smarter, wiser, more com-passionate and more competent than adults. The adults around them are not their equals. Rather, adults are dull-witted, easily fooled, confused and lack common sense. The film is about an omnipotent child in a world of his lessers. There is also a notable absence of friends or peers of Kevin. Like the adults, the children in the film are cardboard standees and lack any real depth like Kevin. He is both all-powerful and truly all alone. How do you imagine that a child who relates to this film feels about taking instruction from a teacher or a parent?

THE ANTI-AUTHORITARIAN GENERATION

Starting in the 1970s, American parents have come from generations whose basic identities have increasingly been characterized by their rejection of, and contempt for, authority. So the last thing many parents today want to be is an *authority figure*. Rather, parents want to be their child's best friend. The need to set firm boundaries, to simply say no to certain things, to administer difficult consequences is all somehow distasteful. Confrontation is shunned as making things more difficult than necessary. Why not reason with children until they see the error of their ways?

However, during the rapprochement crisis a firm authority is exactly what is needed. This authority should be fair, compassionate and without emotional judgment. But it needs to be the authority nonetheless.

An advisor of mine once said that a person of wisdom adeptly moves between strictness and compassion, and between practicality and poetry. Our child rearing has moved away from strictness and practicality and moved toward compassion and poetry. One way this is manifested is in our idealized view of the nature of children. We worship childhood and youth as perfect and without flaws or weakness.

There is a school in Santa Monica, California, called Garden of Angels. While I know only a little about their approach, I suspect that it must be somewhat based on the belief that children left to their own devices would be angels. I've always hoped a school would open across the street called Field of Warriors just to correct the imbalance.

As most parents will attest, children are a bit of both angel and warrior. Children aren't moral creatures, and they aren't immoral creatures, children are amoral. The problem with basing your parenting on the assumption that children are naturally angels is that it places an unreasonable burden on the child and not enough burden on the parent. If we assume that children are angels, then we will naturally be disappointed when they hit someone, or take their toys. Disappointment is judgment and can quickly become a form of manipulation. Everyone resents being manipulated, and manipulation begins a cycle of aggression whether passive or direct. When a parent assumes that children are naturally moral, this excuses them from the burden of shaping their own child's character. The parent who takes responsibility for setting consequences that make it in her child's best interest to behave respectfully, exercise self-discipline and consider others will raise a healthy child. The parent who sets boundaries and consequences without judgment will raise a child who communicates without manipulation or aggression.

For the last eighteen years, many of the children I have chosen to work with have been unquestionably seen as warriors. I like warriors. I admire them. I prefer the warrior to the diplomat. But to be a great warrior you need strictness and compassion, practicality and poetry.

EMBRACE CONFLICT

Moments of conflict and disagreement between a parent and a child, when handled well, are the building blocks for happiness and interdependence. Today's children are more willful, articulate and confident, and conflict with them is inevitable. But more sophisticated children require more sophisticated boundaries. If you fail to set them, or fail to hold them, they will never develop mutual recognition.

WE'RE GOING OUT TO EAT

A mom and dad want to go out to breakfast on a Saturday morning. Their three-year-old says she doesn't want to stop playing with her toys and doesn't want to go. The parents try to convince her that it'll be fun. They complain that it's getting hot in the apartment and speak loudly about how nice and cool it will be at the restaurant. The mom tells her daughter she can order whatever she wants and reminds her about how much she liked the pancakes last time. They tell her she can come back to her toys when they return home. The three-year-old remains unconvinced and steadfast in her insistence that they stay home.

If your three-year-old is making the decisions about when the family goes out to eat, she has too much power and not enough connection. While it's perfectly natural for a three-year-old to try and take control of these decisions, it isn't healthy for her to succeed.

Some parents I've talked with are reluctant in a situation like the above to firmly tell their children to stop playing and get ready to leave. They'll tell me that it feels somehow mean or inconsiderate. After further discussion it's usually the case that the parents associate firm boundaries with emotional judgment and being disregarded.

There's a reason the pendulum swung from authoritarian to permissive parenting. In the authoritarian approach, firm boundaries were set while disregarding the feelings and independence of the child. So when those children grew up and became parents they unconsciously associated firm boundaries with feeling judged and disregarded.

Authoritarian parents who set boundaries while getting angry or dismissive of their children did not know how to deal straightforwardly with their children's natural and healthy assertion of their own will. Consequently, those children became parents who were unable to deal straightforwardly with the assertion of their own will over the will of their children.

The way to straightforwardly deal with children during a conflict of wills is to firmly assert your will while recognizing your child's independence and feelings without judgment:

"We're going out for breakfast so I need you to put your shoes on."

"I don't want to go. I want to stay and play."

"Well I'm sorry you have to stop your fun, but staying home isn't a choice. If you put your shoes on now you can play for two more minutes while Mommy gets ready."

"But I want to play. I'm not going!"

"You have to make up your mind. You can put your shoes on now and play for two more minutes or you can go to time out for two minutes then put on your shoes."

At this point the mom or dad would count to five, and if the girl didn't go to put her shoes on they would give her the time out. The girl might be upset and the parent might add, "I know you're upset. Time outs are a bummer."

Young children require authority figures. Hopefully these will be considerate and benevolent authority figures, but they must be authority figures. Without the child's will coming up against the stronger will of a parent, she cannot transition from omnipotence and into interdependence and she will not develop the healthy tension of mutual recognition.

Children who don't develop the skill to yield their will to the will of the group are going to have great difficulty when they get to school, where it's required, and may end up medicated and marginalized as a result.

NOTES

1. Po Bronson and Ashley Merryman, *Nurture Shock* (New York: Hachette Book Group, 2009), 13-24.
2. Ibid., 20.

Chapter 4

Out of Control Lions

Unlike my approach, which focuses on understanding children's behaviors as largely a product of changeable systems of interaction, a psychiatrist's training is based on a medical model, which focuses on behaviors as a product of neurology and brain chemistry.

DJ THE ISLAND

The 2001 *Frontline* special "The Medicated Child" followed four-year-old DJ and his parents as they tried to cope with his serious conduct disorder. DJ had been diagnosed bipolar because of his extreme tantrums and wild behaviors, and was taking three different medications to try to control him.

On a visit to his psychologist, DJ's mother asks the doctor, "Is there anything not medication-related that we need to be doing for DJ? I mean, is there any type of option? Would he be too young for therapy? Would something like that benefit him if done along with medication?"

The doctor replied, "At this point I think it's like 99% medication. Plus it's harder for him to make use of therapy and to make use of any behavioral program if he's still got a lot of symptoms he really still can't control even if he tried."

Then DJ's mother said, "I just want to make sure that we're doing everything we can." At the end of the appointment DJ's parents left the office with a fourth prescription for medication to control DJ's behavior.

The doctor's response assumed that the only influence DJ's parents have over his behavior is medication and that the effectiveness of any behavior program would depend entirely on four-year-old DJ.

Scenes like this are very frustrating for me to watch because I've seen children just like DJ whose behaviors were transformed through a comprehensive behavior plan. I don't have any ill feeling or judgment toward the doctor or the parents in the above scenario; they are doing their best with the options they have. DJ's parents want the best for their son and so they take him to a person who is recognized as an authority on children's minds. But they need to have other options.

Is four-year-old DJ some isolated island? Do the actions and reactions of his parents have no bearing on the decisions DJ makes, the self-control he exercises and the capacities he develops?

A child like DJ is likely to receive a diagnosis of juvenile bipolar disorder. The diagnosis of juvenile bipolar disorder increased 4000% in the ten years between 1994 and 2003 and often results in children as young as two being given powerful antipsychotic drugs, which have serious side effects.[1] Dr. Jack McClellan, a psychiatrist at the University of Washington, describes the current approach to bipolar disorder as follows, "The treatment of bipolar disorder is meds first, meds second and meds third."[2]

CULTURE OUT OF BALANCE

Our culture has witnessed a tremendous movement away from considering the effects of interactions on child behavior in favor of looking almost exclusively at behavior as a result of pre-established neurology. For this reason I have thrown my entire effort into finding explanations and remedies for behavior in the patterns of interaction. This has always appeared to me a more effective, compassionate and prudent approach.

Whether or not a child has a neurological difference that affects her behavior, shouldn't we always begin with the less invasive and less risky approach of changing the nature of our interactions with her before we begin medicating her? Furthermore, how many children have been medicated for behavior or learning characteristics that would have adapted through a comprehensive behavior program? Only when a scientific approach to reshaping the patterns of interactions has failed to bring enough result should we begin to consider the need for medication.

Today the vast majority of behavior interventions I see aren't comprehensive or scientific. That is to say, behavior interventions are usually done inconsistently, done differently by each individual who interacts with the child, developed without any clear understanding of what's motivating the child's behaviors, and done for such short periods of time that the gradual, yet profound, changes the plan might bring about can never be properly seen or measured. One of the goals of this book is to show the basic steps to remedy this and to begin to design behavior plans that are comprehensive and scientific.

There are tens of thousands of specialists and hundreds of millions of dollars committed to finding the answers to our children's problems in the neurology of our children. I am committed to finding solutions to their problems in the way we interact with them.

In the upcoming edition of the Diagnostic and Statistical Manual of Mental Disorders (DSM-5, the manual that mental health professionals use to determine a patient's diagnosis—to be released in May of 2013), the psychiatric community finally begins to address the tendency to label all severe behavior problems as neurological disorders needing medication. In an attempt to sway psychiatrists away from the overuse of the juvenile bipolar diagnosis, the panel working on the DSM revisions is recommending the addition of a new childhood disorder called <u>temper dysregulation disorder with dysphoria</u>. This recommendation is in response to recent findings that many wildly aggressive, irritable children who have been given a diagnosis of bi-polar disorder do not have it.[3]

MICHAEL AND MRS. DEBORAH

The things children will do and say to get their way have become more extreme. I've worked with three- to ten-year-olds who don't hesitate to hit, spit, kick, bite or curse at you when you oppose their will. The children who are having these tantrums are not intellectually delayed, but are increasingly sophisticated.

A veteran preschool teacher described to me the moment when a difficult three-and-a-half-year-old named Michael finally pushed her over the edge:

> He was running around the room, knocking things over, laughing and refusing to stop. When I finally caught hold of him, I said, 'You need to sit down and listen!' He looked me in the eye and said, 'F**k you, Deborah!' Well, I completely lost it. I couldn't speak. I was so angry I was shaking. He said *that* while he looked me in the eye and used my first name. It was just too much. It was all I could do to keep my mouth shut and hand him to another staff so I could walk out and calm down.

There had been a one-to-one behaviorist with Michael five hours a day for the last year, but she had been using methods that involved trying to teach him right and wrong behaviors by talking and reasoning with him while praising positive behaviors. During this time Michael had only gotten worse.

Michael's teacher Deborah had heard about me and was eager for me to step in. I'd seen a lot of children like Michael, so I told the staff what I expected to happen during that first week. I told them that when I came in on Monday, Michael would throw the biggest tantrum they'd ever seen. "He will act out, I will set a boundary, he'll ignore it, I'll give him a consequence, he will fight it, I will need to hold him, he will have a giant tantrum, and I will wait until he is calm and following my directions before I allow him to return to class," I warned them.

An important note on holding a child: There are several passages in this book that describe physically restraining or holding a child. It is important to understand that before anyone begins a behavior protocol that includes physical restraint, he should be thoroughly trained in methods that assure he can do so in a way that ensures the child's safety. While holding a toddler who is having a tantrum may be relatively simple, it is quite another matter to hold a larger, older, more physically developed child. In either case the utmost care should be taken to ensure the child remains safe and isn't injured when she is being held. Additionally, restraining a child should never be used as a punishment. And because holding a child is often an emotionally charged situation, all efforts must be made to regulate our own emotions to assure that a restraint is done calmly and without anger.

The next day when I came into the class, I sat close to Michael and watched him and waited. After about forty minutes he took a toy away from the boy sitting next to him and when the boy tried to take it back, Michael punched him in the chest. I stepped between them and said to Michael, "You need to take a time out. There's no hitting allowed."

Michael scooted away from me on the floor and said, "No!" As I went after him he started to run away and when I caught him by the wrist he turned and began punching my arm. At this point I scooped him up and held him so he couldn't hit me and carried him, kicking and screaming, to the next room where I could hold him until he calmed down, out of sight of the other children.

I found a place where I could sit and hold him then I took a deep breath and settled down for what I knew would be a long wait. No matter how many times I do this, the first time I have to hold a child is always a bit intense so I focus on calming myself as quickly as possible, knowing my calm will make it easier for the child as well. Michael was screaming and pulling against me, cursing me and threatening me. He would become calm for a moment then begin to rage again. He tried to spit on me, bite me and head butt me. I just waited. He went from angry and threatening to wailing like a baby and back to angry. When he was quiet for a moment, I told him in a quiet voice, "Let me know when you can sit quietly and follow directions," and this spurred another round of angry rage.

After this had gone on for about thirty minutes, Deborah came up to me looking very worried and said, "Joe, I think you need to let him go. This is going on too long!" Michael started to scream and pull even more violently and she said, "He's screaming like you're hurting him and I'm worried what the principal or the other teachers will say if they come by. I think you should let him go."

Michael is getting louder as he hears what's being said, and I say to her, "Deborah, this boy has had this tantrum 100 times before. He's had it in shopping malls. He's had it in restaurants. He's had it in toy stores and supermarkets. He's had it at home so loud the neighbors call the police. He's had it in this classroom. And every time he's had this tantrum someone, at some point, has given up and let him go before he controlled himself, *but not today*. Today I'm going to wait as long as it takes. He needs to have this tantrum."

Michael is screaming and Deborah looks as though she is almost convinced, "I don't know. It doesn't look like it's working. He seems so upset." I said, "Deborah, you've had him for a year and things have only gotten worse. Can you trust me for one week? Just five days. Give me five days with him, and then tell me what you think." "Okay, I guess I just have to trust you," she said, and walked away.

Michael continued to tantrum for another thirty minutes. After an hour he was exhausted and finally quieted down and followed my directions to sit quietly for five minutes until his time out was over. When he was done he went back and joined his class. An hour later he again refused to take a time out and ran away from me while knocking things on the floor. I caught him and held him for a tantrum that lasted almost as long as the first. He went home that day very tired.

The next day was similar to the first except his first tantrum lasted only forty minutes, and his second tantrum only twenty-five. On the morning of the third day he threw his snack on the floor and I told him to take a one-minute time out. He looked angry but got up, stomped over to the time out chair, and sat down. After sitting quietly for a minute he came back to the table, picked up and threw away the food on the floor, then ate the rest of his snack without incident. This was the first time Deborah had seen him take a time out in her class and she got a big smile on her face as she looked at me and said, "I'm going to say it before you can: 'You told me so.'"

Michael had a tantrum a day for the next four days, but they became shorter and shorter as the days went on. After two weeks the tantrums had almost stopped completely. He probably had tantrums that required he be held about twice a month for the next couple of months. Although he still had some problem behaviors, Michael gradually improved all year. By the end of the year he followed most directions and would take time outs when the teacher instructed him to.

FIRM BOUNDARIES MAKE HAPPY, MORE RELAXED CHILDREN

The staff in Miss Deborah's class were surprised that along with having better behavior and following adult directions, Michael seemed happier and more relaxed. He even appeared less anxious and angry with the other children. The staff had assumed he would be more anxious and angry because he wasn't venting his anger or getting his way all the time, but it was just the opposite.

A child who has successfully won his battles with adults over boundaries becomes very lonely, angry and anxious. These feelings then fuel his cycle of acting out and his tantrums. This is because the young child experiences the lack of strong boundaries as abandonment. Imagine the child's tantrums as an expression of his feelings of power and control. These feelings are simultaneously exciting and scary; exciting because they signal his new sense of power and influence, but frightening because he doesn't yet know if others have power like his or if he is the only ones in charge. When a child wins the battles over boundaries, what he learns is that, while he might be the smallest one in the room, he is the only one in control. This is an overwhelming responsibility. When I repeatedly set a boundary that was stronger and more determined than he was, perhaps for the first time in his life, Michael got the feeling that someone else was like him, someone else was in control of things. A weight was taken off his shoulders, and he breathed a sigh of relief.

When I reflected on my experiences with Michael I remembered how the first time I met him he was wearing a "Marvel Villains" T-shirt. His mother said to me, "Michael likes the villains more than the heroes.

He finds the villains more interesting." Of course he identifies with the villains, the villains are the characters who feel all alone, isolated, angry and superior. They act out their anger by trying to control everything and destroying that which they can't control. The villains are the epitome of omnipotence.

Is This Autism?

Not all of the children I work with have violent tantrums. Many of them have learning and attention problems and I'm asked to come in to see what roles behavior and motivation are playing. Usually these children are suffering from omnipotence that has magnified small learning/behavior characteristics into larger ones. The effects of omnipotence don't always manifest in acting out; sometimes they manifest in refusing to act.

William was a second-grader with red hair and freckles. He was taller than most of his classmates, seemed uncomfortable in his body and was reluctant to play any sports. While his peers were beginning to become more socially adept, William was still very awkward in his interactions. William's attempts to socialize with others consisted of short interactions, blurting out wild statements, making strange faces, or acting silly to get attention. Although he was able to have basic conversations with the other students, he seemed impatient with his level of acceptance and was always doing something to draw attention to himself. Ironically, his odd behaviors only served to ostracize him from those whose friendship he craved.

In the classroom he was often distracted by something inside his desk or something going on across the room. He was particularly antsy and inattentive during math lessons and, consequently, was performing well below grade level. He'd had a behaviorist assigned to work with him in the classroom full-time since the middle of kindergarten. While the behaviorist made things more manageable for the teacher, most of William's odd and disruptive behaviors had continued. He'd fallen behind in math and the school was considering moving him from a regular classroom into a special needs class.

When I observed William I noticed how satisfied he seemed with the current state of things. He seemed to enjoy the attention he got from the teacher or behaviorist when he was disruptive. When his attention wandered the behaviorist would prompt him to return to his work. Sometimes he would tell her he wasn't working because he didn't understand and she would help him do his work. Sometimes he would pretend not to hear or he'd change the subject and ask a question about something entirely unrelated: "What time do we go to lunch today?" At one point when she prompted him to return to his work William told her, "You tell me the letters and I'll write them." When the behaviorist said she thought he could do it himself he pleaded, "Please?" When she finally gave him a firm "no" he laughed and reluctantly went back to his work. He often looked amused when, after several prompts, the adults became frustrated. The teacher and behaviorist knew that, unlike the other students in the class, William had difficulty focusing so he wasn't penalized for not finishing his class work. Because of his socially awkward behaviors and perceived impairments of social communication and interaction he had been diagnosed with autistic spectrum disorder.

Both the teacher and the behaviorist acted as though they believed William's behaviors were a result of his inability to learn and attend (as opposed to my view that his abilities to learn and attend were a result of his behavior). Because of their beliefs, the ways they interacted with him functioned as accommodations and crutches that actually enabled the same behaviors they wanted to change.

Out of Control Lions

William's behaviors weren't changing because for him, they were working perfectly fine just as they were. The first thing that needed to change in this dynamic was to move the frustration from the adults to William. His behaviors weren't frustrating to him, only to his teachers. The only way to find out what kind of learning, attention and behavior William was capable of was to create an environment where his current behaviors frustrated him and the only relief from the frustration came when he showed a higher level of focusing, effort and behavior.

William had developed an identity in the classroom and in his relationships with adults that defined him as someone who was not capable and needed help. He externalized his struggles and the adults played their role in taking responsibility that should have been his. This dynamic was evident in the language he and the adults used which assumed he didn't understand what he was doing and the choices he was making. The behavior plan we developed included shifting the language to one that communicated to him he was fully able to understand his choices and their consequences. In this way, the language of the behavior plan shifted the paradigm out of the one that enabled the inappropriate behavior and externalizing of frustrations and difficulties to one that recognized William's independence and abilities to make appropriate decisions.

We set up a behavior plan that eliminated all comments to William about what he should or shouldn't be doing. We replaced these prompts with short time-outs away from his work where he had to sit quietly by himself. Only now we insisted that he finish the work assigned each period, or at least make a strong effort to do so. When he hadn't finished, either because he'd been fooling around or he'd spent too much time in time out, he stayed in when everyone else went to recess until the work was made up.

In other words, we shifted the responsibility for controlling William's behaviors from the adults back to William.

Raising Lions

During the first month using the behavior plan William was kept in for between two and ten minutes four or five times a week. During these minutes he was incredibly focused and sped through any work he hadn't finished. He hated going late to recess and on a few occasions got so upset he cried for a while before he pulled himself together and finished his work. But his behaviors and attention span shifted dramatically and by the end of the second month he only had to go late to recess about once a week. At this point when William was unfocused or inappropriate the behaviorist would ask him if he needed to take a time out and most of the time this alone would refocus him.

His academics were improving, but because he had never memorized his addition and multiplication facts, he was still behind the class in math. I suggested that every day before he went to snack or lunch, he be required to correctly do ten flashcards with addition and multiplication facts. (If he really focused, this took about two minutes.) After two months of this, he knew all of his addition and most of his multiplication facts and the math gap between him and his peers was much smaller. In addition to his academic improvements, William also began to show more restraint in his social interactions. When the behaviorist saw William doing something that might ostracize him from his peers she would tell him to step away from the group for a minute. After the moment away she would ask him if he knew why she asked him to step away. She'd do this without any tone of judgment and most of the time he could figure out why she had asked him to step away. William then appeared to be having fewer outbursts and fewer odd behaviors.

While this intervention may seem like plain common sense, it goes to the heart of a widespread misconception about children: It is assumed that if a child isn't behaving appropriately it's because she doesn't know how to behave appropriately. In truth, all kinds of inappropriate behavior and attention problems can develop because children find it easier and/or more stimulating than disciplining themselves to do the things that are hard. <u>This misconception stems from a belief that self-discipline and self-control will emerge naturally without tension or difficulty.</u>

The behavior intervention with William worked because it created tension. While the behaviorist and the teacher took special care to create this tension without any judgment, anger or moralizing, they shifted the expectations and gave consequences that made it frustrating for William to continue the problem behaviors. When the behaviorist told me that William had cried because he was frustrated by the consequences, I told her I thought that was a good sign. We needed to bring about the changes necessary in William's behaviors as quickly as possible if we wanted to alter the direction he was heading in school. I suggested that when William became frustrated enough to cry, that they compassionately coach him through the consequence rather than remove it.

William's difficulties are another example of too much power and not enough connection. Interdependence, or mutual recognition, is characterized by an internal tension between the child's needs and the needs of others. This constant tension is something that should continue throughout life and is a sign of psychological health. Many of William's inappropriate behaviors were a result of being treated in a way that created too little tension toward connection. The behavior plan we built created tension that pulled William back to center. Although the adjustment was difficult for him, as long as that tension held him in the center, his behaviors, learning capacities and self-discipline grew.

Six months after beginning the behavior plan with William, the teachers and administrators at his school decided he didn't need to be moved to a special needs class.

THE PASSIVE TANTRUM

I see a lot of children like William who are diagnosed with autistic spectrum disorder or mild autism who, on closer inspection, are actually children who are suffering from unchecked omnipotence. These are children whose manipulations and tantrums have manifested as feigning inability or lack of understanding in order to avoid difficult or undesirable tasks and activities (the Passive Tantrum).

The clearest indicator that the child I'm observing is engaging in a Passive Tantrum and not suffering from a form of autism is a distinct inconsistency in the child's ability to understand social interactions and cues from one circumstance to another. If the child's ability to understand social cues and expectations radically improve when she is motivated (doing a preferred activity) and decreases predictably when she is unmotivated (doing an non-preferred activity), then these behaviors are likely a Passive Tantrum that is manifesting in the child pretending not to understand social cues and interactions when it's convenient. These are children who have learned that if they can convince adults they aren't capable of doing something, they won't have to do it.

The problem with treating a child as if she is autistic spectrum when she is really suffering from omnipotence is that these two should be treated in completely opposite manners. With the child who truly has autistic spectrum disorder, the adult should help her understand social situations and interactions. With the child who is actually feigning inability as a means to maintain control, manipulate, or avoid difficulty, helping the child to understand a situation she already understands will only make her attempts to control and avoid difficulty more effective and therefore feed her feelings of omnipotence.

The methods in this book should not be taken as an approach for turning around children with severe autism. Nor do I believe that classical or severe autism should be considered a product of systems of interaction in the home or school. Rather, I believe there is a large percentage of children, like those described in the paragraphs above, who are being misdiagnosed as autistic spectrum disordered because professionals have not been able to find any other effective explanation for their behaviors.

Notes

1. Benedict Carey, "Bipolar Illness Soars as a Diagnosis for the Young," *The New York Times,* September 4, 2007.
2. Benedict Carey, "Revising Book on Disorders of the Mind," *The New York Times,* February 10, 2010.
3. Ibid.

Chapter 5

The Lion's Cage

When the complex behaviors of a willful child go unchecked, it creates a cycle of behaviors that fuels itself and the young lion becomes trapped in a cage of his own making.

Failure to transition fully out of omnipotence and into interdependence can manifest in a variety of ways. A child may have simply developed a set of behaviors that effectively allowed him to avoid difficult tasks and consequently exercise very little self-regulation. William, who was far behind in math because he found it easier and more stimulating to avoid it, exemplifies this. A pattern of this kind of behavior over several years will magnify even minor difficulties of attention, learning and social behavior until the child appears to have neurological problems that can be diagnosed as autistic spectrum disorder, A.D.D./A.D.H.D., or even developmentally delayed. Remember: behavior shapes neurology, not just the other way around.

Another child may have started with a strong inclination toward impulsiveness, precociousness and a need for high stimulation. This child is prone to more severe tantrums and difficult behaviors that might never effectively be contained during the rapprochement crisis. When she gets to school, she is quick to develop a negative self-image and her behaviors escalate. Many of these children are those who could be diagnosed as A.D.D. or A.D.H.D. Children with characteristics that would be called A.D.D. or A.D.H.D. are in perhaps the highest risk group for developing a strong omnipotent identity because of the more sophisticated and tenacious boundary setting that is required in order to contain them and enable their transition into interdependence.

The most extreme manifestation of the omnipotent identity is the child who demonstrates volatile emotions, high levels of manipulation, and severe tantrums. This child has developed an emotionally charged cycle of omnipotence. Her self-identity is firmly rooted in the anxiety-producing viewpoint that she is the most important and competent person in her world. She compulsively tries to control those around her and sees all of her frustrations and difficulties as a result of some unfair or unjust external circumstance or person. These children include many of those currently being diagnosed with juvenile bipolar disorder, and are often given powerful psychiatric medications in an attempt to control their behaviors.

EMMA

Emma was a nine-year-old girl who had a look in her eyes that told you she was taking in more than she let on. She was articulate, pretty and very athletic. She always arrived at school well-dressed in cloths freshly ironed. During a role-playing game that required the children to use play money to pay bills and find jobs, apartments and roommates, a boy named Zach asked her if she would be his roommate. Emma told him if she moved in he would need to pay all the bills. He quickly agreed and she told him she'd think about it.

At school, one moment Emma was charming and engaging and the next she was angry and volatile. When she was angry or disappointed everyone in the room was on pins and needles, waiting to see what would happen next. If she didn't like what she had written she would slowly tear up her paper in little pieces and drop it on the floor in front of her desk. No one was sure what would set her off or how to calm her down.

The Lion's Cage

Sometimes Emma would continue to work on what she had in front of her when the class had moved on to the next subject. When the teacher would tell her to put away her work and take out the next lesson, she would completely ignore him until he put his hand over her work and said, "You need to put this away now. It's time for math." At which point she would say in a condescending tone, "I *heard you* the first time." Then she would ignore him until he spoke to her again, "Can't you see I'm trying to finish!" she'd scream. If you put your hands on her to get her to move she might throw her desk over or run out of the classroom so that you had to chase her. If you caught hold of her before she got out of the room she would scream at the top of her lungs as she tried to bite, kick and punch you. If you didn't catch her until she'd gotten off school grounds and she'd made you run a bit, she might just stop and let you catch her then walk calmly back to school with a smile on her face.

Emma was a perfectionist who earned a leading spot in the school play each year. If she missed a line during rehearsals she would become infuriated with herself and often fly into a rage. If she was agitated or wanted to avoid a subject she found boring she would tell the staff she needed to see her counselor. She'd write a note for the staff to bring to the counselor asking her to come. Sometimes she sucked her thumb and liked to bring stuffed animals to school to set on her desk while she worked.

The staff and her counselors were constantly trying to figure out how to make it through the day without setting her off. When she exploded it took two adults to carry her to a padded isolation room where she would pound on the window with her shoes or fists and scream until you let her out or brought her counselor in to calm her down. Sometimes when her session with her counselor was coming to an end, she would start having a tantrum in the office and would refuse to leave, at which time the crisis staff would have to remove her and bring her to the time-out or isolation room.

Emma had been diagnosed with bipolar disorder and had been given various strong medications, including Lithium and Depakote (a powerful anticonvulsant), with very limited and inconsistent results. Before the behavior intervention I did, she was spending between one and two hours a day in a padded isolation room. Her rages, anxiety and outbursts were escalating month after month and the administrators of the special needs school were afraid she would soon need to be moved to a twenty-four-hour residential school placement.

BIPOLAR OR OMNIPOTENT?

Children with shorter attention spans, a low tolerance for boredom, and who are addicted to stimulation, whether diagnosed with A.D.D./A.D.H.D. or not, will be more difficult to handle during the rapprochement crisis. Their desires and will to have those desires sated will be stronger and consequently, they will push boundaries further and go to greater lengths to get what they want. It should be expected that the tantrums and behaviors of these children will be more extreme and more prolonged than what we've seen from children in the past.

The more extreme and prolonged the demands or tantrum, the more likely parents are to relent and give the child what he wants. When these children get what they want, their sense of their own omnipotence is strengthened, anxiety increases and tantrums develop in their complexity. This cycle feeds itself and will thwart the child's transition from omnipotence to interdependence indefinitely.

As children's behaviors become more extreme, it becomes harder and harder for parents and professionals to see those behaviors as normal and they are more likely to attribute them to a neurological dysfunction.

I believe the forty-fold increase in the diagnosis of bipolar disorder in children during the last ten years is a manifestation of the above cycle. This cycle is also exacerbated by the cultural shifts covered above, as well as ineffective treatment approaches I will cover in the pages that follow.

The doctors and researchers who diagnose children with A.D.D./A.D.H.D. and/or bipolar disorder recognize how closely the two are related. Between 57 and 98% of children diagnosed with bipolar disorder were also thought to have A.D.D. or A.D.H.D., and 22% of the children diagnosed with A.D.D./A.D.H.D. are later diagnosed with bipolar disorder.[1] Many psychiatrists also believe that many children who are diagnosed with A.D.D/A.D.H.D are actually suffering from undiagnosed bipolar disorder.

I believe that the majority of children now being diagnosed with pediatric bipolar disorder, as well as those diagnosed with oppositional defiant disorder, or as emotionally disturbed, are actually showing characteristics consistent with a too-powerful omnipotent identity and the cycles of omnipotence this self-identity breeds.

This out-of-control omnipotent identity can be reversed if you use a program that combines powerful and consistent boundaries to match the will of this kind of child paired with the use of language that supports the child's transition into the interdependent identity.

CHARACTERISTICS OF THE OMNIPOTENT IDENTITY CHILD

Emma showed all the characteristics of a child with a strong omnipotent identity (O.I.). While the O.I. child continues to develop in other areas, their self-identity and the emotional framework from which he views himself and others remains stuck in the omnipotent stage. His tantrums and manipulations become stronger and more complex as he gets older and makes use of more highly developed communication, physical, and cognitive skills. Omnipotence in children can manifest as several or all of the following six characteristics.

1. Manipulative- Emma's feeling that she was more powerful than anyone else, and therefore the person most in control, fueled her anxiety that the world around her was unsafe and that she needed to control it. With each successful power struggle, tantrum or manipulation, Emma's manipulative skills became stronger and more complex. She engaged in manipulation compulsively because it brought her comfort knowing she could control things. However, with each successful manipulation, whether it was convincing her counselor she was too upset to do math or creating so much tension that her teacher ignored her rather than insist she work with the rest of the class, Emma's sense of her own omnipotence increased—and with it, her anxiety of living in a world where she alone was in control.

2. Oppositional and defiant- Emma does not recognize others as equals. Like the Kevin McAllister character in *Home Alone*, she is more competent than all others. Because she has not transitioned to recognizing others as independent and with their own power, her emotional instincts perceive others as either unruly extensions of herself or simply as obstacles to her omnipotent will. She is caught in an emotional catch-22. Because she feels omnipotent, she is alone in the world and responsible for keeping things in control. Her opposition and defiance are another expression of the tantruming child whose hand pushes forward and says, "I'm here and I have power. Does anyone else have

power like me?" She is still trying to gain the recognition that can only be given by someone who has been established as equal to or stronger than she is.

3. Emotionally volatile- the O.I. child has an underdeveloped capacity to process frustration and disappointment and can be quick to break down in tears or fly into a rage. This is due to three factors. First, the O.I. child has placed unreasonable pressure on herself to control everything. Second, children like Emma never made enough of a shift from demanding that things outside of them change (externalizing) to adjusting themselves to deal with frustration or disappointment (internalizing). Because she succeeded in continuing to externalize emotional difficulties, Emma consequently underdeveloped the emotional muscles needed to process difficulties and frustrations. Lastly, emotional outbursts may have been reinforced because they were an effective way to manipulate adults and get them to capitulate to her wishes. In other words, Emma's emotional volatility became an effective tool for exerting control.

4. Inability to accept correction, consequence or direction and/or the need to always be part of every decision. One of the consequences of the current child rearing practice of giving a child a choice about everything is that it reinforces the misconception that children should have control over any decision made that affects them. Consequently, they feel entitled to argue every decision they don't prefer until they are either convinced of the direction or they have convinced the adult to change the decision to accord with their preference. Why should a child who feels

omnipotent take correction, consequence, or direction from an adult she perceives as her lesser?

5. <u>An obsession with everything being fair</u>. One of the difficulties the school staff had with Emma was her constant complaint that things weren't fair. "That's not fair! Hannah was fooling around too! Why do I have to stay in for recess?" "That's not fair, why does Zach get to erase the board! He did it yesterday!" The "it's not fair" argument was both a compulsive response to anything Emma didn't like and a manipulation to get what she wanted. She was so astute at finding flaws and inconsistencies in those around her that when we started using a behavior plan at school she would complain to her mother any time a staff member didn't follow the script exactly. "I wouldn't have gotten so upset if Felicia hadn't said she was sick of me. You shouldn't be able to say that to kids. She should be fired." I would get calls from her mother relaying exaggerated tales of what the staff said or did that wasn't perfect and were the cause of Emma's outbursts. This behavior is a consequence of allowing a child to continue to externalize problems and frustrations. The once healthy tendency of the infant to look to the caregiver (seen as an extension of them) to meet all her needs and resolve her frustrations (make everything fair) grows into an inability to accept any disappointment or difficulty. If Emma felt frustrated or unsatisfied with a situation or outcome, she assumed that the source of the problem was external and unjust (unfair) and should be changed to relieve her discomfort.

6. <u>Perfectionist tendencies</u>. Emma needed to be the best speller in the class in order to feel secure because of her belief that every-

thing was up to her to control. She placed enormous pressure on herself to do things perfectly. This was fueled by the anxiety that comes from feeling that if she didn't control things they would be out of control. Because she won the majority of power struggles with her caregivers, she perceived herself as not only most powerful, but also the most responsible for keeping things safe.

In order to turn Emma around, stop the cycle of omnipotence and enable her to transition into Interdependence, I set up a program that created the holding environment she didn't have between ages one to three. This holding environment, however, was stronger and more sophisticated to deal with the complex omnipotent identity that Emma had developed by age eight and with her considerable intelligence.

The behavior program I set up trained all the staff Emma interacted with at the school to work in unity. The staff actions and the language they used were choreographed and scripted. Inappropriate and oppositional behaviors were met with 100% predictable consequences and specific language used by all the staff. Seven staff members at the school were trained in Emma's behavior program. These staff rehearsed and choreographed their parts together and role-played handling common scenarios. Only the school staff members trained in the program were allowed to interact with Emma when she became oppositional or inappropriate.

The first day the behavior program was put in place, Emma's behaviors escalated to the most severe we'd seen. She spent three hours raging in the isolation room. The second day she was in isolation for two hours. By the end of two weeks she was spending on average less than an hour a day in isolation and by the end of ten weeks she was spending only an hour a week in isolation. All violent and physically aggressive behavior stopped after four months.

Eighteen months after the start of the behavior program, Emma was doing well in a regular public school class, unmedicated and without any special accommodations, where she has remained without incident for almost three years.

The behavior program I designed for Emma was a system of interaction designed to develop the psychological muscles she wasn't using, replace her unhealthy patterns of interaction and perception with healthy ones, and bring about a shift in her self-identity. These programs can be designed for a single behaviorist at a public school, or for a group of staff in more difficult cases like Emma's. (See chapter 9 for more on these programs.)

MANY PATHS TO OMNIPOTENCE

There are at least two ways a child's sense of omnipotence can be strengthened and develop into a cycle of problem behavior fueled by anxiety. First, in a normal home with too much power and not enough boundaries. Second, in a neglectful or chaotic home which lacks structure, consistency and control from the adults. In this second case, the cycle begins with the anxiety a child feels because of the lack of control and structure. The child tries to control an unsafe chaotic home environment through exerting their will wherever possible. Their omnipotence and anxiety grow as a result of their successful tantrums and this feeds their sense of power. It should be noted that the child whose omnipotence developed because of a neglectful or chaotic environment is less likely to exhibit the last two qualities of the omnipotent child: <u>An obsession with everything being fair</u> and <u>perfectionist tendencies</u>.

The adults parenting these children often feed the cycle of omnipotence because they respond with either the *smash the hand* or the *avoid the hand* parenting. The child will experience boundaries that are either permissive and indulgent, or authoritarian and judgmental. When boundaries are enforced, it is done harshly with yelling, judging and perhaps hitting: "I'm tired of this, you little brat! If you do that again, I'm going whip your behind!" When this parent isn't authoritarian, she is instead overindulgent and permissive because she is parenting from guilt and shame caused by her negligence and inappropriate parenting.

When the parent is authoritarian, the child feels negated and power-less. This causes him to act out in order to experience a feeling of power. When the parent is permissive, he experiences this as abandonment and he acts out in order to assert control. In neither situation does the child experience the mutual recognition necessary for him to feel truly recog-nized, and so the acting out continues.

A child exposed to this kind of parenting may likely develop cycles of omnipotent behavior that would become increasingly difficult and extreme. Eventually a child like this may end up being diagnosed and medicated and/or sent to a special school for difficult children like the ones I often work in.

DAVID'S FIRST DAY

Recently a ten-year-old boy named David was admitted to one of the schools I work with. He was lean and a bit small for his age. He was well dressed with khaki pants, a button-down shirt and a belt. He was a bright young man who liked to play Hangman and always wanted to be the one to make up the word to guess. About an hour and a half into his first day of school, he got into a fight with another boy and when the staff tried to break it up, he hit the staff and screamed at them and they had to carry him to the isolation room while he thrashed and screamed. Once in the isolation room, he continued to scream obscenities and hit staff. Despite the staff's attempts to calm him, his behaviors only got worse. He tried to force his way out of the isolation room, spit on the staff and hit the Plexiglas window with his fists and shoes. These behaviors continued in waves for about two hours, at which time they came to get me.

Before I went into the isolation room I talked with the staff member who was already there. He told me what had happened and I asked him to get two chairs and be ready to bring them into isolation on my cue.

When he was ready I went into the isolation room and said to David, "I need you to have a seat right there (pointing to a spot on the floor). If you are not sitting there in five seconds I'm going to hold you. 5... 4... 3... 2... 1... " When I got to 1, David moved in the opposite direction from where I'd indicated and sat down.

This was his first test for me. If I allowed him to move in the opposite direction he would have established that his will was stronger than mine, that my unequivocal direction was actually negotiable. If he could get me to relent, even just slightly, from following through exactly as I said then he'd have set a precedent for our interactions. I knew I needed to set the precedent that I do *exactly* what I say I will do.

When he sat down in the opposite direction I signaled for the two chairs and I put David in one chair and I sat in the chair behind him and held him. He resisted being put in the chair and kicked and cursed at me. Initially, he screamed obscenities and threats: "I'm going to f**king kill you mother f**ker! I'm going to stab you in the head if you don't let me go motherf**ker!" These threats went on for a couple of minutes while he thrashed around in the chair.

In a silent moment when he was taking a breath I said to him, "When you're quiet I'll tell you what I need from you if you want me to let you go." I don't think I was able to finish the sentence before he started cursing and flailing again.

The Lion's Cage

After this he began crying and flailing his head around and screaming, "You're hurting me! I can't breath! Let me go! You're killing me!" His eyes were red and he was screaming hysterically, "Let me go! It hurts, it huurrttss! It huurrttss! I can't breath! You're holding me too tight! I can't breath! You have to let me go!"

I checked how I was holding him to make sure he had enough room to breath and I noticed that when I did loosen my hold he would only pull and twist against me more vigorously. I said to him, "If you are pulling and trying to kick me I've got to hold you tighter," and, "I can't let you go until you've stopped your tantrum and are following directions." Again, before I could finish speaking he was yelling. This time he yelled, "I can't stop until you let me go! Let me go you motherf**ker!"

At this point in the tantrum, I need to summon up my conviction and faith. Even though I'd been through this kind of tantrum a couple of hundred times with different children, the first time I have to hold a child is never easy. It is only through coming up against an unyielding will that is stronger than his own will, that he can begin to transition out of omnipotence. If I give in, compromise or negotiate with him, then he won't learn to use the emotional muscles of self-control I know he has. In a sense I am giving him more respect than he has ever gotten before because I'm communicating to him, through my actions, that I believe he can control himself; that he is not broken or disabled. I know if I can wait him out, if I can remain calm, if I can keep using language that lets him know I believe he can control himself, when he's ready to, then he will pull himself out of his tantrum and exercise self control, not because I took away the difficulty, but because he made the decision to do so.

By setting and holding a firm boundary, even in the midst of his tantrum, while simultaneously using nonjudgmental language that affirms his independent power to choose his actions, I am leading him into mutual recognition.

As David's tantrum continued, he started to try negotiating: "Look motherf***er, let me go and I'll follow directions! What the hell's wrong with you! Help me! Someone help me! This f***er won't let me go! You're hurting me, you f***er!" His screaming and crying continues as well as his attempts to pull himself loose from my hold. His tantrums are coming in waves of anger and threats, pleading, asking for sympathy and hysterical crying.

His tantrum had been going on for about twenty minutes at this point and the other staff in the room (it was his first week at the school) looked a little freaked out. So I said to the staff, "This boy has probably had this tantrum a hundred times and each of those times he has escalated or continued until the adult gave in or gave up holding the boundary. But today that's not going to happen. Today he's going to exercise self-control."

At this point in my intervention the most important thing for me to do is to quietly hold him and wait. Every couple of minutes when David was quiet for a moment I'd say to him in a calm, almost disinterested tone, "Let me know when you're finished with the tantrum and I'll let tell you how you can get back to class."

I know that a boy who is having a tantrum like this is used to having someone *talk him down* or *de-escalate* him. This usually entails telling him to take deep breaths and reassuring him everything will be all right. Sometimes it will also include helping him to process what is going on or making some concessions and negotiating with him. In some scenarios, a therapist might even take him away to play a game or draw to help him calm down. But I believe any of this, while perhaps shortening that particular tantrum, will inevitably prolong the problem and feed the roots of it.

The Lion's Cage

One of the important shifts that must occur in order for a child to shift out of omnipotence and into interdependence is learning to internally process frustrations and difficulties. In order for this to happen, the adults must allow the child to hold these struggles for himself. A child who is still in omnipotence after age four has most likely learned that adults will hold, process, and sometimes eliminate his frustrations and difficulties for him. The problem I have with verbally de-escalating a tantruming child is that it denies the child the opportunity to do it for himself. David was stuck in a maze and I needed to let him find his way out by himself. If I step in and show him the way he will expect the same thing next time. If he can get others to handle his difficulties and frustrations, this will inevitably feed his sense of omnipotence.

From the first interaction I have with a child, I want my actions and inactions to communicate to them, "You are entirely responsible for, and completely capable of, controlling and calming yourself. And I will wait as long as it takes for you to do so."

David was still flailing and screaming after thirty minutes, so my hands and legs started to get a bit sore at this point. If his tantrum continued for more than an hour I'd let another staff take a shift holding him.

After about forty-five minutes, quite suddenly, David stopped resisting, sat quietly and began following my directions. I told him, "I need you to sit quietly, without resisting while I hold you for five minutes. After that you will sit quietly in the chair without me holding you for five minutes. Do you understand?" David nodded his head, "I need to hear your words." "I understand," he said. At this point I continued to hold his wrists but hold his arms more loosely and I say to him, "There are four steps you need to take to go back to the classroom. First, sit for five minutes while I hold you. Second, sit for five minutes on your own. Third, come outside the isolation room and sit quietly. And fourth, do five minutes of class work to show you're ready to go back. If at any point during these steps you don't follow directions or are disrespectful then you start the steps again from the beginning. Do you understand?" David said, "Yes."

After we sat in silence for five minutes I told him, "Okay, your first five minutes is finished, so if you're ready, I'm going to let you sit quietly without me holding you for five minutes. Are you ready to start?" He told me he was, so I let him go and he sat quietly.

These stages of sitting quietly are important because they develop just those emotional muscles that he didn't use which resulted in him coming to the isolation room. I also want to build on the precedent we had established that he could indeed exercise self-control.

Although it can be emotionally and physically draining to hold a child during this kind of tantrum, it is also deeply satisfying to see him turn that corner. Moments of conflict with children are also opportunities for deep connection. I may well be the first adult that has not allowed this child to win the battle for omnipotence. In her book *The Bonds of Love,* Jessica Benjamin says, "The painful result of success in the battle for omnipotence is that to win is to win nothing: the result is negation, emptiness, isolation."

When I have waited as long as it takes for a child to fully recognize me, and the boundary I've set, I have communicated to them, perhaps for the very first time, that they are not alone. The constant "fear (of) the emptiness and loss of connection that accompanies his fearful power" is at last relieved. His world has suddenly become a little safer, his anxiety is diminished, and he begins to feel a new sense of connection to others.

Perhaps because he went through this on his first day at our school, David never again needed to be taken to the isolation room. Although he was still very oppositional and during the next month or two, he had some outbursts and needed to be walked to the time-out room, he never needed to be physically restrained again. (He had needed to be physically restrained regularly for the previous five years.) His classroom teacher had a very consistent classroom protocol using the principles in this book and David adapted very quickly and was soon thriving. A few weeks later he asked me to teach him to play chess on his breaks, which I did.

In my experience it is unusual that a child will completely stop their violent tantrums after only one experience like the one above. Most children who have violent tantrums like David's require more than one physical intervention. The more typical response is a gradual fading of tantrums over subsequent days or weeks.

HOLD THEM NOW OR HOLD THEM LATER

While the necessity of regularly physically restraining a child over the course of several days, weeks or months may seem harsh, it must be compared to the more common practice of medicating these children. The drugs used to treat children with severe behavior problems and a diagnosis of bipolar disorder, oppositional defiant, or emotionally disturbed are typically of three types: mood stabilizers, anticonvulsants and antipsychotics. Some of the common side effects of these medications include sedation, drooling, slowed speech and thought, fatigue, tremors, drowsiness, dizziness and weight gain.

Although some may eschew the necessity of physically restraining a child, our culture appears to have fully embraced the use of chemical restraints to manage children's behavior. While physically restraining a child should never be used as punishment, it is both a necessary and compassionate part of a therapeutic intervention plan for a child with violent and/or aggressive behaviors.

If parents use a Meet the Hand parenting approach with their children and hold firm boundaries, even if this means holding their child beginning when the child is a toddler, then it will not be necessary to physically restrain them later on. The longer a parent waits to set and hold firm boundaries, the greater the chance that the child will have an overdeveloped sense of omnipotence. If parents wait until a child is four, five or six years old to firmly enforce the boundaries they set, their child's sense of omnipotence may be so strong that it will appear that the only way she can be managed is with drugs.

THE POWER OF DOING NOTHING

One of the most powerful instincts I brought to my work with children is the capacity to remain calm and do nothing. Don't get me wrong. I may be holding the child at that moment, or she may be sitting in a time-out chair that she knows she can't leave until she has remained quiet, but the most important thing I'm doing in that moment is nothing. It is only when I'm doing nothing that the child can develop the emotional muscles necessary to handle her difficulties internally. When I am calm and relaxed while she is struggling, she will slowly develop the capacity to mirror these emotions when she struggles through these things in the future.

Remaining calm, waiting and doing nothing communicates something much more powerful than talking or giving the child something to sooth her would. It communicates faith and expectation that the child can and will navigate her way through the difficulty and frustration she's experiencing. I can't count the number of times when I've been called in to consult on a particularly difficult case, only to find that when the child reaches the critical moments of tantrum and/or difficulty, someone is always stepping in and taking the obstacle away from the child in order to calm and sooth her. Consequently, the child never learns to calm and sooth herself and the problem behaviors continue.

The Lion's Cage

For instance, when Sarah would become aggressive and out of control, the crisis staff would take her to the time-out room to calm down. Usually a trip to the time-out room required the student sit quietly and follow staff directions for ten minutes before returning to class. But if Sarah's screaming and demands to be released from the time-out room got too loud or continued for too long, her counselor was called and she was taken on a walk around the school so she could calm down before going back to class and the boundary of sitting and following directions was not held.

This is an extension of what Jessica Benjamin termed the inability to have faith in your child's "ability to survive conflict, loss and imperfection." Except instead of this lack of faith being simply a struggle of a solitary mother, it has become the predominant opinion of our culture. Parents are besieged by marketing that tells them their children are in constant danger of developing this or that shortcoming unless the parent is vigilantly attending to their every need.

The behavior problem child, the autistic spectrum child, the A.D.H.D. child, the oppositional-defiant child—all will test the limits of your faith in their ability to survive conflict, loss and imperfection. Because these children are filled with a sense of their own omnipotence, they are more willful than children who have come before them and they will go to much greater lengths and extremes to win power struggles. The solution is to shift our faith and expectations. Maybe our parents only had to wait out a tantrum that lasted five minutes and we will have to wait for twenty minutes, but we must wait.

One of the important things for most parents to remember is that even children who are not on the more extreme end of characteristics such as willful, stimulation-driven and oppositional are going to have a significantly longer and more difficult rapprochement crisis than children had thirty or forty years ago.

Don't Fill the Void

We want to create a space that is structured and controlled by the adults in which a child can process himself through difficulties and develop and exercise self-regulation. Allow the consequences of his decisions (time outs, removal of stimulation, and refusal of adults to give too much attention/reinforcement to his tantrums) to shape his behaviors and choices.

When guiding a child through a tantrum or frustration, there are moments when the child will not know what to do or how to solve his problem. This is a void, an empty space, that the adult must resist filling. These moments require waiting and faith. Waiting for the child to fill this void and faith that the child can and will survive this frustrating and confusing moment. To fill this void for the child, to solve the problem that the child might have solved given time and faith, is to rob him of the creative moment in which he fills this void himself and discovers his real power. Your faith and calm during these moments when your child is facing this void become the model for the calm your child will internalize when facing difficulties, frustrations and his own imperfection in the future.

NOTES

1. Rif S. El-Mallakh and S. Nassir Ghaemi, *Bipolar Depression: A Comprehensive Guide* (American Psychiatric Publishing, 2006), 108.

Chapter 6

The Language of Lions

Recently, a third-grade teacher named Stacy told me the following story and asked me if I thought she'd been too harsh with one of her students. She'd been teaching a lesson with the children sitting on the floor in front of her when Jeremy raised his hand. When she called on him he asked a question that was entirely off topic and she told him, "That's not what we're talking about so I'm not going to answer that." A few minutes later Jeremy raised his hand again, and with a smirk, again asked an entirely off-topic question and Stacy told him the same thing. After a few more minutes Jeremy did the same thing again. This time Stacy had had enough and she told Jeremy, "You know, I think it's very disrespectful for you to keep interrupting this discussion with questions you know have nothing to do with what we're doing and I don't appreciate it." A few of the other students could be heard giggling quietly. Jeremy looked a little embarrassed but still seemed amused by it all.

After she told me the story I asked her, "Do you think Jeremy understood that his question was off topic the first time he asked it?" And Stacy said, "Yes, I think he did know. He definitely knew the second time. Socially, he's very astute."

Then I asked her, "Do you think he knew it was disrespectful to keep interrupting you with these questions?" And Stacy said, "Yes I think he knew it was disrespectful. But I think he just didn't care. He thought it was fun."

THE MYTH OF NOT KNOWING

There is a myth that if children aren't behaving appropriately it's because they don't know how to behave appropriately. As a result, when children misbehave adults explain things that children already know. But explaining something to a child that he already knows, or speaking in a manner that infers as much, will develop a dysfunctional communication dynamic, feed omnipotence and breed manipulation.

When I started to work with children, I often saw this dynamic between teachers and students in the classroom and between parents and children in the home. Adults were constantly telling children rules and boundaries they already knew. Over the course of some years I was able to break down this dynamic so as to better understand it, reverse it and create motivating interactions.

If you listen to what's said in a classroom or at home, you can divide the inappropriate behaviors into three types, and the responses to those behaviors into five types. The three types of behavior are benign, malignant and impulsive.

Benign behavior – five-year-old Mia leaves kindergarten class to go to the bathroom without asking or telling anyone because she didn't know the rules. Benign behavior occurs because the child doesn't understand the behavior is not acceptable (positive intention).

Malignant behavior – eight-year-old Tony throws a paper airplane at another student while the teacher's back is turned. Malignant behavior is behavior that the child understands, or could reasonably figure out, is not acceptable (negative intention).

Impulsive behavior – A student calls out the answer to the teacher's question without raising his hand because he is excited that he knows the answer. Impulsive behavior occurs as a reaction to something or as an impulse without any time to think. The child understands the behavior is unacceptable but acts before thinking (no intention).

There are five types of responses to problem behaviors: Information, Action, Ignore/Accommodate, Question and Inappropriate.

Information response – The teacher says to Mia, "Leaving class without permission is not allowed. If you need to leave the class, then ask me so I know where you are." An information response is a response that gives information. (Give information.)

Action response – After he throws the plane, Tony is told he needs to move to a desk in front next to the teacher. This is a response that requires an immediate action or delivers an immediate consequence. (Give a consequence.)

Ignore/Accommodate response – The teacher can see by the look on William's face that he realized he should have raised his hand before calling out, so she ignores his outburst and continues her teaching. Some behaviors are minor enough to ignore, and others, like squirming around in your seat or needing to stand or pace, can be accommodated so they are not disruptive. (Allow the behavior.)

Question response – Dana is talking to Abigail while her teacher is trying to lead a lesson so her teacher says to Dana, "Dana, do you need to move to another seat?" (Ask the student to make a choice.)

Inappropriate response – "I'm sick of telling you to shut your mouth when I'm teaching." There are an infinite variety of inappropriate responses to children including yelling, insulting, sarcasm, threats and rhetorical questions. All of these build a pattern of disrespect and should never be used.

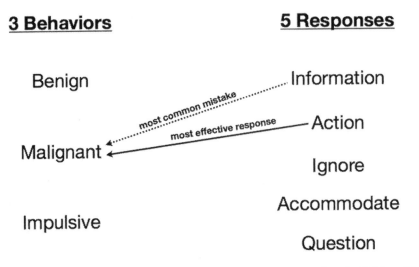

3 Behaviors

Benign

Malignant

Impulsive

5 Responses

Information

Action

Ignore

Accommodate

Question

most common mistake

most effective response

Each of the three behaviors above has responses that build healthy communication with children and responses that undermine them.

ONLY BENIGN BEHAVIOR NEEDS INFORMATION

The only time an information response is necessary is with benign behavior, because this is the only inappropriate behavior that stems from lack of information. Having said that, I would estimate that perhaps 1% of inappropriate behaviors I see in classrooms are benign. In other words 99% of problem behaviors are behaviors that children know, or can easily figure out, are inappropriate.

Just imagine that you could stop the action the moment after a problem behavior and you said to the child, "I'll give you $100 if you can tell me what you just did that I have a problem with." In my experience, 99% of the time, with a little motivation, children know, or can easily figure out, what behaviors are inappropriate.

Parents and teachers typically know when a child does something he knows is inappropriate. A mother of a two-year-old recently told me, "I can see in his face he knows he's not supposed to do it, but he does it anyway. He *knows* he's being naughty." Despite the fact the child knew what he was doing was wrong, the mother still responded by telling the child that what he was doing wasn't allowed, perhaps because she didn't know what else to do.

In order to develop children who are the protagonists in their own learning, children who don't wait to be told something, but take the initiative to learn it, we must restrain ourselves from telling them those things that they can figure out themselves.

RESPONDING TO A LION

What I suggested to Stacy (the third-grade teacher responding to the constant interruptions of Jeremy) was the following: Instead of repeatedly telling Jeremy what he was doing wrong, then finally lecturing him about his disrespect (*information responses*), give him a consequence that takes all the motivation and fun out of doing it (*action response*). The second time he interrupts you (or the first time if he's made a habit of it) tell him, "Stand up, please. Have a seat on the carpet behind the rest of the group and sit quietly." After a few minutes, ask him, "Are you ready to rejoin the group?"(*question response*). And if he says yes, allow him to rejoin the class without mentioning the behavior.

Lecturing Jeremy about the behavior he knows is disrespectful is condescending. Additionally, he finds the negative attention from his teacher, and the positive attention from his peers who think he's funny, entertaining. When you move him away from the group and don't talk about the behavior, you've taken away the reinforcement for, and the judgment of, that behavior and treated him with the respect that communicates your high expectation of his abilities to understand and correct his behavior.

Information Responses Invite Argument & Manipulation

<u>In the home</u>
Mom – "Daniel, I've told you I don't want you going on the Internet if I'm not in the room."

Daniel – "But you let Michelle go on by herself. Why can't I?"

Mom – "Your sister is seventeen years old. You're nine."

Daniel – "But I promise I'll only go on the sites you say are okay."

<u>In the classroom</u>
Teacher – "Jimmy, keep your hands to yourself."

Student – "But Evan keeps copying me!"

Teacher – "Evan, stop copying Jimmy."

Student 2 – "I'm not copying! Jimmy keeps bothering me."

When you give an information response to behavior, you invite manipulation and/or an argument. If you're a teacher, you end up wasting valuable lesson time on something that is potentially more exciting to the problem student than your lesson, thereby providing the negative reinforcement she was looking for as well. Keep this can of worms closed.

Once you get the children in your classroom or home used to the fact that you give short reasonable consequences and won't engage them in arguments about who did what, all the manipulation, wasted time and negative reinforcement stops.

A sure sign that a classroom or a home is dominated by a tone of disrespect is when the adult in charge is using too many information prompts. If the number of information prompts in response to inappropriate or disrespectful behavior outnumbers the number of action prompts then you're sure to have a lot of behavior problems. The overuse of information prompts is the biggest single problem I see in the breakdown of respect and cooperation in a home or classroom.

WORDS MUST BE PAIRED WITH ACTION

Unlike older or more sophisticated children, toddlers need to be given information about what the rules are. One-, two- and three-year-olds are learning the rules for the first time, so it's important to explain the rules. They will learn the rules faster and are more likely to believe and adhere to them when there are clear consequences attached. When a child doesn't know, or if you're not sure they know, what behavior is expected, give a small consequence while telling them the rules. Walk them to the time-out space while you tell them, "If you hit your sister then you need to sit in time out for two minutes."

If it's a behavior you want to stop, like tantruming, you can begin giving them the consequence while explaining how their choice (cause) is leading to the particular effect—like in the "Faith Needs a Nap" section in chapter two, when I let Faith know that if she can't stop tantruming, she'll have to have a nap. Additionally, it is important for teachers and parents to use good judgment when they see any child who is sincerely confused about a situation or a consequence and take a moment to help her to understand. The biggest problem with giving a consequence isn't the consequence itself; it's the emotional judgment and/or anger that often accompany it. If there is no judgment attached to the consequence, then you can coach your child through the consequence as the natural cause of the choice she made and not as a punishment for being "bad."

MALIGNANT BEHAVIOR NEEDS ACTION

Malignant behavior should be responded to with actions, or sometimes, a question. When Tony is caught throwing the paper airplane, he is told to move to the desk at the front of the room for the next five minutes. In this way there is an immediate negative effect for the problem behavior.

Giving action consequences in response to malignant behavior goes to the core of understanding why problem behaviors occur. Problem behaviors occur because, on some level, *they work*. They give that child something he wants. If they didn't work there'd be no motivation to do them. Maybe throwing the airplane is more stimulating than the lesson. Maybe the consequences for getting caught throwing something are negligible. Maybe there is a generally disrespectful dynamic between Tony and his teacher. Maybe Tony likes being the center of attention, even if it's negative attention.

The point of responding to malignant behavior with an action—a real consequence—is to change the result of the behavior from one that works to one that doesn't work.

When we react with anger or judgment to a child's inappropriate behavior, we have forgotten that children choose these behaviors because, on some level, the behavior gets them what they want or need.

INFORMATION IS VAGUE. ACTIONS ARE NOT.

The definition of acceptable behavior changes from class to class, from home to home and from home to school. In one class, if Tony threw something he'd spend the rest of the period in the office and an hour in detention. In another, the teacher would tell him to please stop and would continue teaching. Children learn very quickly that words mean different things in different situations; they get their meaning from the actions that are associated with them.

For behaviors that children understand, or can easily figure out are unacceptable, there must be real consequences to their actions, otherwise the boundaries and rules become meaningless. These consequences should be reasonable and administered without judgment.

Children are concrete thinkers. Lofty concepts and ethics hold little or no significance if they aren't backed up by experiences and facts. Imagine that, in one room, a teacher tells his students, "Talking while I'm talking is unacceptable," but gives no consequence. Every time he says this to the students in response to someone talking over him, the power of that statement gets weaker and loses meaning.

Now, imagine another teacher who never once tells the students that it's not acceptable to talk while he's talking, but every time it happens he has the student doing the talking get up and move to another seat or he keeps her for a few minutes after class. He may never have said, "Talking while I'm talking is unacceptable," but in his class, this is a fact.

If the toddler in your home is hearing lots of information about what's allowed and not allowed ("No throwing olives, Jacob") but there are no consistent consequences to match those words, all he is learning is that the words you're using have very ambiguous meanings.

TOO MUCH EXPLAINING IS DISRESPECTFUL

The way we talk with children places so much emphasis on the importance of words and communication and so little on consequences that today's students believe when they are praised by a teacher it means they are doing poorly, not well.

> Psychologist Wulf-Uwe Meyer, a pioneer in the field (of studying the effects of praise), conducted a series of studies where children watched other students receive praise. According to Meyer's findings, by the age of 12, children believe that earning praise from a teacher is not a sign you did well—it's actually a sign you lack ability and the teacher thinks you need extra encouragement. And teens, Meyer found, discounted praise to such an extent that they believed it's a teacher's criticism—not praise at all—that really conveys a positive belief in a student's aptitude.[1]

While the communication dynamics can be complex, the "what to do" is simple. **Use action responses in 99% of situations and stop telling children what they did wrong.** The hesitancy people have with giving consequences is that they don't want to be unfair and they don't want to pass judgment. But if you learn how to give effective consequences, neither of these should ever be a problem.

GAVIN'S POSSE

One afternoon I was at the recreation field of a large middle school, visiting one of the behaviorists I was training, when I saw a student bullying other students. He walked into the middle of a group playing basketball, followed by his two friends, and grabbed the ball and kicked it away. When someone said something, he pushed his chest out and got in the face of the kid who'd complained. Then he gave the kid a threatening push and walked on to another group where he smacked an unsuspecting kid in the back of the head. When the kid turned around he again challenged him to a fight, at which point the kid threw up his hands and walked away (malignant behaviors). As he continued his rounds in this way I asked the behaviorist if he knew this kid. He told me the boy's name was Gavin and explained that all the kids were afraid of him and he was constantly bullying them.

So I walked up to Gavin and said, "You need to have a seat over there for five minutes." (action response) He looked at me dismissively and said, "S**t, I don't know you." And he started to walk away.

I said to him, "Right now you've only got a five-minute problem. But if you don't have a seat you'll have a much bigger problem."

He turned and started walking slowly toward the bench I'd indicated and said, "What did I do! Man! At least tell me what I did."

So I told him, "Okay, I'll tell you what you did, but it'll cost you another fifteen minutes because I don't like wasting my time. So I can tell you what you did and you can sit for twenty minutes or you can sit for five minutes *then you tell me* what you did." (question response)

He said, "Fine, I'll sit for five minutes," as he walked over and sat on the bench.

"I'll come let you know when you can get up," I told him.

Five minutes later I went up to him and said, "So tell me why I asked you to sit down." (question response)

He looked at me and said, "Because I hit that kid in the back of the head."

"What else?" I asked. (question response)

He thought for a moment and said, "I kicked that basketball."

"What else?" I said. (question response)

"Um... I don't know... I can't think of anything else."

"I guess that's enough. You can go." (action response)

When he got up, Gavin and his friends went to the far opposite side of the recreation fields.

The point of the five-minute time out was not punitive but rather a deterrent. I wasn't interested in punishing him for what he did. I was interested in him not doing it again. If I'd seen it happen again I would have had him sit for considerably longer. If the behavior had not stopped completely I would have continued to increase the consequence until it was sufficient to stop his behavior. If Gavin hadn't sat down or had walked away from me I would have gone to the dean and arranged a one-hour detention. That way, the next time I asked him to sit for five minutes he'd do it.

MEETING GAVIN'S HAND

You can also understand my interaction with Gavin from a Meet the Hand perspective. Gavin had become an expert at establishing dynamics that were either avoiding the hand (permissive) or squashing the hand (authoritarian). When staff avoided confronting him because he was such a handful, or they allowed him to give an excuse/apology for his behavior, they were practicing Avoid the Hand child rearing. When staff did firmly call him out on his behavior it was usually accompanied by an angry lecture and over-the-top consequences, so they were using Squash the Hand child rearing.

I believe the anger that drove Gavin to bully others was in part the result of the isolation he felt at not having his will firmly met by the will of another. Gavin was craving the connection that is only really made during a Meet the Hand interaction. He needed someone who would set a reasonable boundary, firmly and without any condescending or insulting interaction. He needed the connection that happens when one will firmly opposes another in a respectful manner: *Meet the Hand.*

Bullying at School

On January 14, 2010, fifteen-year-old Phoebe Prince committed suicide after suffering months of constant bullying from school classmates. This was only the latest of a string of extreme bullying incidents becoming more prevalent in public schools.

The continued increase in the frequency and intensity of bullying is a result of several things. First, there has been a cultural shift in today's children toward much stronger feelings of omnipotence (a strong self recognition and a weak recognition of others) than in children of the past. One of the consequences of this is that children feel a stronger pull toward satisfying their own needs and feelings than respecting the needs and feelings of others. Combine this with the lower capacity for intimacy (due to the lack of healthy mutual recognition) and a child's already strong desire for social status and power, and the result is more children who are willing to be cruel in order to impress and belong to a group.

The third problem is our assumption that bullies act in ways that are inappropriate and cruel because they lack an intellectual understanding about right and wrong. So we respond with conversation (when school bullying gets out of hand therapists are sent in to talk with children about the effects of bullying and why it is wrong). Bullies don't lack a cognitive understanding of why their actions are wrong. The truth is they are acting this way because on some level it gets them the social power they crave. If we respond to bullying with swift, strong consequences that reduce their social power, instead of more talk, then bullying will stop. Moralizing to them only makes the gap between you and them wider and feeds the "cool factor" of their social power with their friends.

In order to stop bullying it is necessary to respond with action consequences that remove the incentive as soon as the first signs of bullying appear. When this is done swiftly and consistently, then a culture of bullying won't have a chance to take root and grow, never mind grow to the levels of cruelty we've recently seen at our schools.

The short version: respond to bullying immediately with more action and less talk.

FIFTEEN RULES

I wince whenever I go into a classroom where the students pretend that if the teacher hasn't told them specifically not to do something then they can't be held accountable for that inappropriate action. Often these classrooms have fifteen rules posted on the wall spelling out items that are just plain common sense ("No hitting or physical aggression," "No cursing," "You must have the teacher's permission to leave the room," "Be polite," "Raise your hand to speak," etc.) The effect of posting so many rules is to communicate to the entire class "My expectations of your abilities is extremely low!" Or more to the point, it tells them, "I believe that my students have no common sense. So go ahead and act that way!" Inevitably, these classrooms are difficult to manage.

WHO FIGURES OUT THE RULES

I prefer not to even talk about classroom rules and expectations, but rather when an inappropriate behavior occurs, I give a short, non-judgmental consequence, and follow through 100% of the time. For instance, on the first day of class a student throws a wad of paper at another student (malignant behavior) and I tell him, "Marlon, stand up please." (action response)

"What?"

"Just leave your things there and stand up." (action response)

"What did I do?" he asks as he stands up.

"Don't worry, you're not in trouble. But I'll need you to leave your things at your desk and have a seat at that empty table for a couple of minutes. Thank you." (action response)

Then I return to teaching and after a couple of minutes I turn to Marlon and ask, "Are you okay to go back to your desk?" (question response)

"Yes"

"Okay, go on back." (action response)

What this dialogue communicates to the students is, "You're smart enough to figure out and understand the rules of my class. I have a high expectation of your abilities. If you do something that I have a problem with, I won't judge you or lecture to you; rather, I will administer a brief consequence, and you will learn and adjust your behavior." Very quickly the class assumes a respectful demeanor. I take responsibility for setting and keeping boundaries and they take responsibility for their behaviors and dealing with the consequences of those behaviors.

I like to set up a dynamic where children have to be on their toes. Where they understand that they're expected to figure out what the rules are. If sometimes this frustrates them, it's an opportunity for me to calmly and kindly coach them through difficulty, to let them know I have faith in them and it's okay to struggle and to fail. In a world where children are constantly condescended to, students quickly adjust and find my interactions with them very mature and respectful.

Action consequences require the child to immediately do something. The most common example is requiring a child to move to another seat for a minute or more. The child can be asked to move to a special desk (I usually call this the "focus desk") or simply to move to a desk near the teacher for a moment. If they're outside playing, the action may simply be to sit down for a few minutes. At home an action consequence could be turning off the TV, leaving the game room, forfeiting their cell phone for an hour or taking a two-minute time out in a quiet chair. An action consequence temporarily interrupts the child's access to stimulation.

DEALING WITH IMPULSIVE BEHAVIOR

Impulsive behaviors are the behaviors that children do without thinking. Calling out the answer *and then* raising their hand, constantly moving, hands always fiddling with something, and having difficulty staying seated are all examples of impulsive behavior.

When responding to impulsive behavior you have three responses to choose from. You can choose action, ignoring or accommodating. The first thing you have to ask is, "Is this behavior disruptive?" If it's not disruptive to either the student's learning or to other students' learning, then the behavior can be ignored or accommodated. If it is disruptive, then you can respond with a short action consequence. Short action consequences in response to impulsive behaviors that are disruptive will serve to create a small bit of tension around the problem behavior. This in turn will motivate the child to be more aware of, and exert more effort to control the behavior. In essence, you are bringing him into an awareness of mutual recognition.

I remember training a young teacher named Jackie who had a class of behavior problem third-graders. There was a boy named Tyler who was both emotionally volatile and could almost never sit still. His squirming around got worse when it was harder for him to concentrate. During math each day he would constantly change his position in his chair. First he'd fold a leg underneath him and sit on it then perhaps the other leg. Then he'd sit cross-legged on the chair or he'd lean the chair back on two legs, then perhaps balance the chair on one leg.

Tyler's constant moving during math drove Jackie nuts and she was constantly asking him to sit properly. The more comments she'd make about his sitting the more irritated he'd get until, by the end of the lesson, (if he was still in the classroom by then) they were both very annoyed with each other. Quite often Tyler would get so irate by the middle of the lesson that he was angry and disrespectful or gave up trying to participate and just ignored the lesson. But this would cause other problems, as Jackie would then ride him about participating in class.

I told Jackie that this was a battle she didn't need to fight. While Tyler's squirming might seem improper during class, the truth was it wasn't causing any problems. He was able to participate in the lesson despite his constant moving and no one other than the teacher seemed disrupted by it. This was behavior that could be ignored or accommodated. She could ignore it and go on teaching or, if it was disruptive, she could accommodate the behavior by having him sit behind the other students during math, so as not to disturb them.

The next day Jackie ignored Tyler's squirming and kept teaching without any comments to him. At one point Tyler was standing behind his chair leaning over with his elbows on his desk while he listened to the math lesson. But Tyler remained engaged, participating in the lesson and doing his math work. When the lesson was over, Tyler had finished his work, was respectful and in a good mood. Jackie was also in a better frame of mind because she hadn't spent the lesson trying unsuccessfully to get Tyler to sit still.

I checked in with Jackie two weeks later and she told me that Tyler was doing much better during math class. He was participating, finishing his work and talking to her in a respectful tone. Tyler's performance all day showed improvement once his teacher learned to ignore or accommodate those behaviors that didn't need correcting and learned to give action, not information consequences for those behaviors that were disruptive.

Many teachers and parents struggle when dealing with impulsive behaviors. The ability to discern between behaviors that are simply unusual and those that are clearly disruptive or malignant is essential to dealing effectively with them. The teacher or parent who knows which behaviors should lead to consequence and which behaviors to ignore, and reacts to both without any judgment, will develop healthy, respectful relations with these children.

ONE STEP FURTHER: CREATIVE ACCOMMODATION

A sixth-grade teacher in Minnesota named Abby Brown designed an adjustable desk to accommodate her student's work preferences. Rather than insisting that children sit still, she lets children in her class stand and fidget if they prefer. The stand-up desks come with swinging footrests, and with adjustable stools allowing children to switch between sitting and standing as their moods dictate. Both the teacher and her students say the adjustable desks help them concentrate.

"Sometimes when I'm super tired, I sit," said eleven-year-old Nick Raboin. "But most of the time I like to stand."

"At least you can wiggle when you want to," said Sarah Langer, twelve.

Teachers in Minnesota and Wisconsin say they know from experience that the desks help give children the flexibility they need to expend energy and, at the same time, focus better on their work rather than focusing on how to keep still.

- From The *New York Times*, by SUSAN SAULNY, Published: February 24, 2009

LOVE IS NEVER ASKING THEM TO SAY "I'M SORRY"

Most parents and teachers regularly ask children to apologize for things they've done. When one child hits another I'll commonly hear, "Apologize to your brother! There's no hitting allowed. Now say you're sorry." Then the one will sheepishly say to the other, "I'm sorry." Children quickly learn that apologies are a cheap currency with which they can pay for their inappropriate, impulsive or bad behavior.

I was in a third grade classroom the other day and saw six girls in two groups playing a math game when suddenly I heard a girl say to another, "You are so stupid! Why did you join my team?" The teacher overheard the exchange and said, "Abi, we do not allow that kind of talk in here! Do you want to sit on the bench for recess again?" Abi shakes her head "no" and the teacher continues, "How would you feel if someone called you stupid? You owe Sophie and me an apology. I don't allow those words in my class." Abi then says, "I'm sorry Mrs. Johnston. Sorry Sophie." When the teacher walks away Abi turns to the other girls in the group, gives them a little smirk, then resumes playing the game.

In the above interaction it's as if the teacher had said to Abi, "Because you behaved in a way I find inappropriate you'll need to do two things. First, lie to me. Second, lie to the girl you've insulted. Okay, now continue playing."

We need to understand that children operate from a perspective that is based on cause and effect. What children find most important is social power, not right or wrong or good and bad. When Abi insulted Sophie she was throwing around her social power, not acting out of some misunderstanding of the rules of the class. Abi knew the rules of the class better than the teacher.

But Mrs. Johnston did "allow those words"—she just required a small payment in the form of the lie "I'm sorry."

Don't Require an Apology

Rather than solicit or force an "I'm sorry," you should model sincere apology. We feel compelled to get apologies, yell, prove the child wrong and us right because we suffer from the delusion that the world operates by the laws of right and wrong rather than the laws of cause and effect.

Asking a child to apologize as a consequence is another form of moralizing and manipulation. Action consequences should not include requiring the child to apologize or say she won't do it again. Whether a child is actually sorry has to do with whether she was motivated to do the behavior and if she will be motivated to do the same behavior again in the future. Children take actions based on self-interest. It is up to the adults to ensure that problem behaviors do not serve the interests of the child. When the adult has done their job of making sure inappropriate behaviors have no reward, then the child will naturally stop doing them.

Not Sorry at All

One of the practices that is closely tied to telling children to apologize is penalizing a child at school by having them write standards. The definition of standards is those morals, ethics, habits, etc., established by authority, custom or an individual as acceptable. Teachers often assign a student to write them down as punishment for misbehaving such as writing, "I will not throw things in class" one hundred times.

One day while I was training the time-out staff at a school, a boy named Devon came in with the classroom aide, angrily sat down and started to kick the wall. The aide who brought him in said he was re-fusing to write standards and showed me his paper. In small letters on the top line he'd written "Im sorry fore actig inaproprecly" and below in large letters he'd written "IM NOT SORRY AT ALL." The aide told me that Devon was supposed to write, "I'm sorry for acting inappropri-ately" twenty times.

There are many problems with having students write standards. First, it operates under the misconception that students act out because they don't understand right from wrong. Students act out because it works, so when you treat them as if they don't understand, you create a condescending dynamic.

Second, standards create a negative association with schoolwork. Kids who are acting out probably already have a negative experience of schoolwork and this is in part why they are acting out. The last thing they need is to be punished with sitting and writing over and over again that which they already know.

Third, you can't control or manipulate a child to feel what you want him to feel. At least Devon was honest enough to refuse to write what he didn't believe.

Fourth, when you ask a child to tell you he's wrong over and over again, it is humiliating and initiates a strong oppositional dynamic. For children who have difficulty taking direction, this is the emotional equivalent of adding gasoline to a fire.

Fifth, when a teacher tries to direct a child to have a feeling he doesn't actually have, she is shirking her responsibility. If you want Devon to actually be sorry for how he behaved, then it is up to you as the adult to make the consequences for those behaviors worse then the rewards. Set up consequences that are sufficiently strong and there will be no need to try to force Devon to say he's sorry. He'll feel it.

THE BALANCE OF MOTIVATION

Most information responses to inappropriate behavior are by their very nature negative and condescending. They remind the student what he is doing wrong. On the other hand, short action consequences given without any judgment are either neutral because they don't address the behavior, or positive because they infer high expectation. While consequences might be difficult, or even frustrating, they shouldn't be paired with judgment that the child's decisions are right or wrong. All these comments accumulate in the mind of the child to form the image of how he imagines you perceive him.

If you look at all of a teacher's or parent's comments and place each one in a category of either positive, negative or neutral, you can see whether her relationship with the child is more likely to positively or negatively motivating.

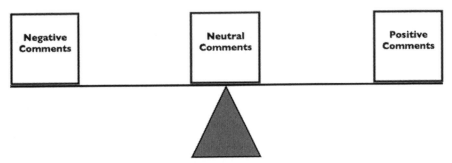

I was training a behavior specialist named Alicia who was working with a particularly difficult ten-year-old boy named Peter. When she was working with him in the classroom she was constantly correcting him. Peter would be fiddling with something in his desk and she'd say, "Peter, I need you to put that away." Thirty seconds later it was, "Stop playing with your eraser," and then, "If I need to tell you again to get started you're going to miss recess time." This went on and on throughout the day. There were short periods when Peter would become focused and attentive but most of the time Alicia was constantly riding him about all that he was doing wrong.

The constant barrage of corrective/negative comments piled up like weights on Peter's shoulders and served to develop his negative self-image in the class and fuel his motivation for further inappropriate behaviors.

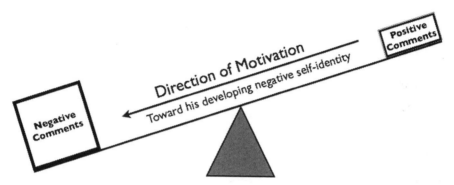

I asked Alicia to completely stop giving any comments about Peter's behaviors. I explained to her that, rather than commenting on the behaviors, she should only refer to consequences. I explained how, when she comments on Peter's behavior, she feeds a dysfunctional dynamic. I asked her to only use one of two responses to inappropriate behavior. Once she decides that the behavior must be addressed then she should either respond with, "Do you need a break?" or "Please take a one-minute break."

Not only did I want her to eliminate all comments or corrections on Peter's behavior, I also wanted her to eliminate any tone of judgment from her voice when delivering the two action prompts above.

I asked Alicia that after each comment or prompt she gave to Peter, she ask herself, "Could you tell from my response whether I approved or disapproved of his behavior?" If the answer is yes then it was potentially de-motivating and feeding the dysfunctional dynamic. If the tone of voice used when the prompt "Do you need a break?" communicates any judgment then the prompt is less effective. Imagine that the prompt was recorded and played to someone who wasn't there. Would they be able to tell whether you were responding to behavior that you disapproved of?

By shifting the way she talked to Peter, by changing the negative information messages to neutral action prompts, Alicia would effectively shift the balance of motivation and create a positive and more joyful classroom setting for Peter.

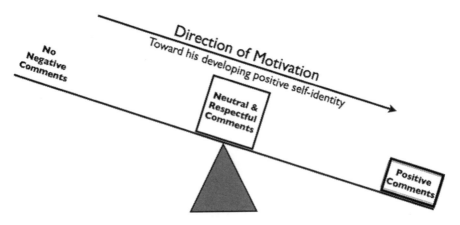

Using this approach forces the adult to rely solely on the effect of consequences to shape behavior rather than judgment, shame, praise or other emotions. Let the consequence do the work.

"I HATE POLITE CHILDREN!"

I remember sitting in a kindergarten class when all the children were on the carpet while the teacher read to them. A little girl had asked the teacher something after which the teacher announced in a loud voice, "Did you hear the way Kristen said that! That was *so* polite. I *love* polite children."

Immediately, the five-year-old boy I'd been sent in to work with said in an equally loud voice, "I *hate* polite children!" The teacher was livid and I quickly took Jimmy outside the class to sit for a time-out.

Jimmy was a handful. During his first six weeks of kindergarten, all three of the behavior specialists who'd been sent to work with him had quit. He would run away, hit or spit on you when you tried to hold him, he couldn't sit still for a moment, he always seemed angry, and he could dish out the sarcasm and insults like a road comic. But Jimmy was also tender, articulate and funny—more so than the other children. He could tell when people didn't like him; he just didn't understand why. He had a brother who was three years older, well behaved, better looking, more athletic, polite and clearly his mother's favorite.

It probably didn't take Jimmy long to realize that the rules at school weren't much different than the rules at home. If you were polite, could sit still and keep your hands to yourself and focus on what people told you, then the teachers liked you, you were praised and your skills were applauded. But if you were impulsive, funny, said the first thing that popped into your head and had a hard time concentrating on the thing in front of you, like Jimmy, you were constantly being corrected, the teachers were annoyed by you. You were always in trouble.

If you know you're in a situation where you'd never win, why not have some fun? Perhaps you can at least leave with your dignity. Jimmy knew he was "the bad kid." Under these rules, even with his greatest efforts he would only be a below average polite kid. Why not be the best bad kid? At least there's some pride in that.

THE BAD BOY IDENTITY

The point of Jimmy's story is that styles of classroom management and communication play a major part in how children view themselves, and therefore how they behave in a classroom. A child who struggles to succeed in school, whether because of attention or learning differences, is much more likely to develop a negative self-identity at school. For instance, a child who has no problem focusing on activities that involve building and moving but has great difficulties focusing on activities that require sitting and listening is likely to get a lot of negative feedback about their performance at school. "Mia, put the crayons away and pay attention." "Mia, sit down and wait for me to call on you." "Mia, leave the models alone and find a book."

Watch these children in the classroom and count how many times they get comments correcting or criticizing vs. how many comments praising or approving of what they are doing. If a child receives ninety correcting or criticizing comments to every ten praising or approving comments, that child will have a negative self-image in that classroom. Even if the teacher is making special efforts to praise, that child will begin to learn that who she is in that classroom is mostly wrong. If this continues for a while the child will begin to feel that, at school, she is a bad girl.

This negative self-identity can lead to a child giving up trying to seek approval and accepting the role of the bad girl/boy in the classroom. By the time I came into Jimmy's kindergarten class, he had so many impulsive and destructive behaviors going on that the teacher was correcting or criticizing him every sixty seconds. Jimmy's negative self-image was so strong that he identified with the villains, not the heroes, in cartoons. He liked to be the one doing the chasing, would pit himself against five or ten other children, and he reveled in the power of frightening others. When he would play with the other children at recess he would insist on playing the role of a dark tyrant like Darth Vader or the evil transformer Megatron. Villains in cartoons and movies epitomize individuals with powerful omnipotent identities. They view themselves as alone, superior to others and they crave complete control over everything.

SHIFTING IDENTITY

One of the biggest challenges for teachers and behavior specialists who work with behavior problem children is turning around the child who has developed a negative self-identity at school. It's not difficult to see how a negative pattern is established and how the cycle feeds itself and grows. A child doesn't perform well in school. The majority of messages that child gets are corrective, the child becomes discouraged and rebellious. The child begins to feel belligerent and acts out even more. The teacher is more riled and reacts more emotionally, which feeds the negative acting out.

Turning this dynamic around can be especially difficult. A teacher or behaviorist who gets this student has got to overcome a situation where the vast majority of the student's behavior is negative and disruptive. If for instance 90% of a student's behaviors are inappropriate and need correcting, while only the remaining 10% are appropriate, how is it possible to create feedback to that student which is positive and motivating without ignoring all kinds of behaviors and setting a precedent of "no boundaries?"

The usual scenario with a child like this is that the teacher or behaviorist gives 90% corrective or negative messages and gives 10% affirming or positive messages. The net result is that the child is negatively motivated. The child sees himself as a sum of the interaction with that adult. The adult in this situation can tell him, "I think you're great" or, "You've got a lot of ability" or, "You can do anything you set your mind to" or any number of generally praising remarks about the child—and none of this will matter if 90% of the things he actually does are reacted to with corrective/negative messages.

A willful child is going to assert their power and personality. Whether it's as Darth Vader or Luke Skywalker will depend on how he perceives himself reflected in the eyes of those around him.

EQUATION FOR A HAPPIER AND MORE MOTIVATING HOME OR CLASSROOM

- Eliminate 90% of your information responses to problem behaviors.
- Ignore half the behaviors you used to comment on.
- Give action consequences in response to 90% of the behaviors you address.
- Follow through 100% with each consequence.

Your children will feel less berated about their actions. They will accept the consequences you give because they are short and reasonable. They will argue less because you always follow through. You will feel respected because your children take you seriously. And your home or classroom will be much easier to manage.

NOTES

1. Po Bronson, "How Not to Talk with Your Kids," *New York Magazine,* February 2008. http://nymag.com/news/features/27840/index2.html.

Chapter 7

Lion Training

THE "STRAW THAT BROKE THE CAMEL'S BACK" METHOD

Imagine a young mother who tells her three-year-old son Nathan, "If you behave and listen to Mommy, then you can go to the movies with Daddy tonight." But the boy keeps acting out, throwing things and not listening to his mother. Each time he misbehaves his mother tells him, "Nathan, unless you start behaving you're not going to the movies with Daddy." After the fifteenth time telling him she finally says, "That's it, I've had enough. You are not going to the movies with Daddy tonight." A three-year-old experiences a verbal warning as no real consequence so the series of events looks to them like this:

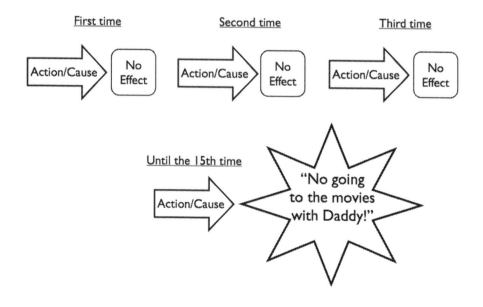

The conclusion that three-year-old Nathan reaches is, "Most of the time there is no consequence for not listening to Mommy." And, "Sometimes (one time in fifteen) Mommy gets mad and takes away something I like."

MAKE CONSEQUENCES IMMEDIATE

Instead of giving big consequences after "the last straw," it is better to give lots of small consequences that are given after each problem behavior. Then your child is learning, "There is always a consequence for not listening to Mommy."

Children are observing what's happening around them and trying to draw conclusions about how things work and the meanings of words. If fourteen out of every fifteen times a parent says "No throwing your toys," or "Hitting your brother is not okay," there is no consequence paired with the rule. The child learns that most of the time the rule isn't true. If your two-year-old drops the toy and goes away crying every time your four-year-old hits him and you give no other consequence than telling him that hitting his brother is "not okay," what he's learning is that your words are not true. Hitting his brother is okay because when he does it, his brother drops the toy and goes away—which is what he wants.

The most effective immediate consequence is the short time out. A short time out is a simple means of assuring that problem behaviors are not reinforced or rewarded. A short time out can be given in a classroom, the home, on a hike or while out shopping.

When you stop a child and give them a short time out you're ensuring that the most immediate effect the child experiences as a result of their behavior is boredom. You effectively stop any reward or stimulation that the child is getting from the inappropriate behavior and replace it with a short period of nothing to do.

Short immediate consequences also make it easier for your child to begin to manage their own behaviors. It's easier for children to control themselves when dealing with a one or two-minute time out than it is for them to deal with a long time out or a big consequence. Additionally, it gives your child a better opportunity to exercise control over those actions that are leading to larger consequences.

SOPHIE'S DANCE CLASS: LEARNING TO CONTROL IMPULSIVE BEHAVIOR

A client used the above principles with her three-year-old daughter, Sophie, at dance class. Sophie looked forward to her weekly dance class and would put on her dance outfit and dance around the apartment talking about the instructor, Miss Sarah, a couple of days a week. But when she was at dance class she would get over- excited and silly and refuse to follow Miss Sarah's directions. She'd climb onto the stage and refuse to get down or she'd get out the Hula Hoops when the class was doing something else. Her mother tried taking her outside to have her calm down, but after a few minutes back in the class she was over-excited and out of control again. Her mother would warn her that if she couldn't listen to Miss Sarah they'd have to go home. After warning Sophie repeatedly and even taking her out for ten minutes to calm down, her mom would take Sophie home in tears. They had been to four dance classes and hadn't made it through to the end of one yet. Jennifer wasn't sure Sophie was ready for this class and was debating whether to throw in the towel.

I suggested that she try a couple more weeks using the following program: If Sophie wasn't listening or was becoming out of control,

Jennifer would ask her to come over and sit next to her quietly for one minute. After the minute was over she could rejoin the class. If Sophie didn't come over, or refused to sit for a minute when asked, then Jennifer would take her into the hall to sit two minutes quietly, followed by sitting for the one minute inside before rejoining the class. I suggested that she be willing to do this ten or more times each class to see how Sophie adapted.

I encouraged Jennifer to use language that helped Sophie understand the connection between her actions and the consequences. "If you're not listening to Miss Sarah then you need to have a one minute break. If you sit quietly next to Mommy for one minute you can go back and dance with Miss Sarah." And, "If you don't come when Mommy calls you or I have to chase you then we have to have a time out in the hall. After the time out you can come back in, sit for one minute next to Mommy, then go back and dance with Miss Sarah."

The first week Jennifer gave Sophie eight time outs, half of which were in the hallway. The second week Sophie needed eight time outs again, but only one in the hallway. On the third week Sophie needed six time outs, all of which were in the dance room. In other words, Sophie was following Jennifer's directions, coming to her and taking the time outs when asked. In the weeks that followed Jennifer gave Sophie anywhere between two and five one-minute time-outs per class. But this seemed a small price to pay for allowing Sophie to participate in a class she so looked forward to. After all, she was able to participate in at least fifty-four minutes of each hour-long class, not to mention that the tears and disappointment of having to go home and miss dance class ended.

The most important thing for Sophie's development wasn't the dance class; it was learning how to exercise self-control. The regular use of short consequences allowed Sophie to gain gradual control over her impulses and slowly develop self-regulation at the rate she was able.

Lion Training

GIVE SHORT, REGULAR CONSEQUENCES

Short time outs are most effective for several reasons. First of all, short time outs are less likely to get an argument or a struggle. Although at first children are likely to test the seriousness of the time out through pleading or negotiating like, "I'm sorry. I won't do it again," or, "Please? I'll be good. I don't want a time out." Sometimes children might simply refuse and have a tantrum. So initially it requires some tenacity on the part of the adult to enforce exactly a quiet, obedient one-minute time out. Once the child realizes that the time out is always consistently enforced, and that it is always short and relatively easy to do, then you will begin to get consistent cooperation. So the second reason short time outs are effective is that they are relatively easy to do.

The first goal of any behavior management system is cooperation, so consequences for behavior should be gradual and natural and not punitive or excessive. When consequences are gradual and natural it is easier to administer those consequences in a neutral, or good-natured tone like a coach rather than in an emotional tone like an opponent.

Giving short consequences is much like an air conditioner gives short periods of cool air to maintain a comfortable room environment. So if you want to keep the room around seventy-four degrees, you don't wait until it's ninety degrees in the house. Rather you give a short period of cooling off when the temperature goes to seventy-six degrees.

Here's the third reason to give short easy-to-do consequences: behaviors are easier to manage when you deal with them before they get too hot. Rather than waiting until you've given a child fifteen chances/warnings and then having to give a big consequence ("No movie with Daddy tonight!"), give immediate consequences that are shorter, easier to give and easier to do.

Manage your consequences so that too many consequences naturally lead to bigger consequences. For instance, in classrooms that send children who are misbehaving to a focus desk (no work or anything else is allowed at the focus desk) for periods of a minute or two at a time, the natural consequence of going too often is that any class work that isn't completed as a result must be done by the student at their next break, free time or recess. So a student that has spent fifteen minutes of a forty-five-minute lesson at the focus desk might miss the first part of recess, finishing the work the rest of the class already finished. When the student is upset with the teacher because she can't leave for recess right away, it is easy for the teacher to remain the coach and point out the cause and effect rather than punitive nature of the natural consequence: "Don't blame me. I'd like you to go to recess as soon as possible too. But if your work isn't finished like everyone else, you have to stay in until it is done."

In the case of three-year-old Nathan throwing his toys and going to the movies, his mother can tell him that before he goes to the movies he must clean up his toys and take his bath. Only if these things are finished by five o'clock will they have time to get to the movie. Short time outs can be given so that if Nathan is constantly misbehaving he will not have done what was required by five o'clock to go to the movies. In this way you set up a pattern of small consequences that allows Nathan control of how things go. You also set up a situation that allows you as the parent to coach your child through the consequences as a natural effect of their choices, "I'm sorry Nathan, I wish you could go to the movies with Daddy. But you refused to pick up your toys and it's past five o'clock."

When you give immediate, easy-to-do consequences, you are shaping your consequences to fit the attention span and psychological muscles of your child. Giving big consequences after many accumulated actions is like asking them to lift a fifty-pound weight. Whereas giving short, regular consequences is like asking them to lift a five-pound weight ten times. The psychological muscles of self-control and self-discipline will develop quickly with regular, easy-to-do consequences and, step by step, the child will move from undisciplined feelings of omnipotence into the balanced, self-regulating interdependent identity.

GIVING AN EFFECTIVE TIME OUT

A simple time out is sitting quietly in a chair for a minute or two. If a child is upset and crying when in time out, I say to them "Let me know when you're done crying and we'll start your time out." Because a time out shouldn't start when a child is crying. She needs to get control of herself first. Part of the consequence when a child loses control should be regaining it. A one-minute time out might take ten minutes, nine minutes crying and one minute sitting quietly. Sometimes I will also add, "It's okay to cry. When we're upset sometimes we need to cry. But the time out can't start until you're finished."

One of the common problems that render time outs ineffective is letting the child scream, cry or tantrum during her time out. If you send your daughter to time out for two minutes and she sits and cries during the entire time, she hasn't had to exercise any self-control and is still out of control when she leaves the time out. Time outs shouldn't start until your child is sitting quietly and has gained control of herself. You want to require your child to exercise self-control in response to her not exercising self-control that caused the time out in the first place.

When you have a three–year-old, you might give thirty timeouts a day. Each time you give her a short time out, you're giving her a moment to exercise self-control even if just to sit quietly for one minute. You're letting her build the muscles of self-regulation a little bit at a time.

Most time outs should be very short—one or two minutes. If the child goes right back to the problem behavior, then send her right back to time out, saying, "Oh, I guess you need to have another time out." If she keeps acting out, then keep giving her time outs. Eventually, this will frustrate her and she'll make a different decision.

There's no need to cajole a child into calming down. Allow her to be upset. You want to let her know that sometimes we make bad decisions and that's okay, because we want our children to be willing and able to take risks. "I understand you're upset. If I had to sit in time out three times I'd be upset too. But you make your own decisions. So next time you can make a different choice."

Another typical difficulty that people have when they give a time out is that they spend the time out time talking their child through it in an attempt to help her to understand or to comfort her. The problem with this is twofold. First, talking to your child during time out makes it a stimulating, not a boring consequence, so it reinforces the behavior you trying to stop. Second, it denies her the opportunity to exercise her muscles of self-control on her own.

The impulse to comfort and over-explain a consequence comes from an adult's natural difficulty watching a child struggle or be frustrated, perhaps an inability to believe in the child's capacity to survive frustration and difficulty. But difficulty and frustration must be experienced if the child is to successfully develop the psychological muscles needed to transition into Interdependence and mutual recognition.

CORPORAL PUNISHMENT?

You may have been able to spank a lamb,
but it won't work with a lion.

A young woman named Jessica told me a story about something that happened when she was six that she has never forgotten. Her father had brought her with him to visit his friend, who had a four-year-old daughter. At one point Jessica was left with the four-year-old in the girl's room and told by the fathers, "Make sure she cleans up this room." After a few minutes of the little girl refusing, Jessica decided to give her a spanking because that's what her father did to her when she didn't do what she was told. The fathers rushed into the room when they heard the screaming to find that Jessica had the four-year-old over her knee and was spanking her with a book. When her father told her she wasn't allowed to spank other people even if they don't do what you say Jessica asked her father, "Then why do you spank me?" At this point Jessica's father brought her into the other room and spanked her. Needless to say Jessica went to bed that night very confused.

Corporal punishment doesn't work. Honestly, if I thought that it was an effective means of raising children who were respectful and self-disciplined I'd be for it, but it isn't and I'm not.

I often hear parents ask me, usually in hushed tones, How come spanking seemed to work when they were children or when their parents were children. Fifty years ago spanking a child had a very different result than it does today. That's because children fifty years ago were being raised differently in many ways. Fifty years ago children weren't empowered and treated with the same kind of respect and consideration that we treat our children with today. Those children didn't have the sense of their own power and entitlement that today's children have. (Not all entitlement is bad; for instance, it's a good thing when a child has the belief that he is entitled to be treated with respect and not beaten.) Fifty years ago most children hadn't been encouraged to stand up to adults who were treating them unfairly, and an occasional spanking may have been an effective consequence.

Today corporal punishment always creates more problems than it solves. In an age when we raised children who had only a little sense of their own power, it was a bit more effective, but with today's children it will always backfire on you. Don't use it; it's the last tool used by a frustrated parent who has run out of ideas. You're the adult. Find another way to give a consequence. If you need more ideas, keep reading.

"The first man to raise a fist is the man who's run out of ideas."
– H.G. Wells

Instead of spanking, use boredom. Boredom is your friend. Removing access to stimulation is the humane tool that can replace spanking.

JAMES

I was recently working with a boy named James who had just turned five. James was articulate and very smart and seemingly impossible to control. At his day care center he decided to see what would happen if he unrolled an entire roll of toilet paper into the toilet and flushed it. The director of his day care center said one day during naptime she watched him stand next to a sleeping girl with his foot raised over her hand, as if to step on it. He looked around to see who was watching him and saw the director, he paused a moment as they looked at each other, then slammed his foot down just next to the little girl's hand. The director rushed over and said, "James, what are you doing? You could have hurt her!" James just smiled at her, enjoying the attention and said, "I wasn't going to step on her hand."

James had been thrown out of five day care centers already and the school district had assigned a full-time behavior specialist for his first year in pre-K. James would refuse to follow adult directions, had daily tantrums and had hit, kicked, cursed and spat on adults and other children. Because of his angry and violent behaviors toward staff and peers, the teacher and the behavior specialists told his parents they thought he should be diagnosed as emotionally disturbed.

If James was engaged and interested in something, he gave it his full attention. But if he were at all bored by what was going on, then he would find a way to make trouble. During these times he seemed to need redirection every fifteen seconds. "James, keep your hands to yourself," "James, put that back," "James, don't say that." And for every redirection, James had a smart answer: "Why? But I wanted to paint it red." "But Taylor isn't doing what he's supposed to." "But he already has two papers." Sometimes he would just say, "Sorry" with a knowing smile and then do it again a moment later, and then say, "Sorry" again.

When I first observed James in pre-K, he was sitting on the carpet and the teacher was reviewing the class rules. As she read the rules to them they were asked to repeat them after her, "Eyes watching," "Voice quiet," "Body still," "Ears listening," and, "Hand raised when we want to talk."

James was listening and fidgeting around at the same time. He didn't wait for the teacher to say the next direction and instead repeated the one she said and said the next one before she could say it. The teacher said, "Eyes watching" and everyone repeats, "Eyes watching", except for James who said, "Eyes watching, voice quiet." Then she said, "Voice quiet" and James said, "Voice quiet. Body still." The teacher ignored him the first two times he did this, then told him to only repeat the one she says. James agreed but as soon as she said the next one he did the same thing again.

Between instructions and reading ahead, James is also turning around to tell the boy sitting behind him, who hasn't learned to read yet, what he should be saying. When the other boy gets it wrong, James corrects him then laughs. The other boy gets mad and eventually leans forward and punches James.

By the time the lesson is over James has been given a "red" which means he must miss the first five minutes of recess. When recess starts, his behaviorist sits talking with him. At one point the behaviorist says, "If you'd listened to the teacher you'd be outside playing right now." James says, "That's okay, I like it inside." When the five minutes are over and the behaviorist tells him he can go out, James says, "You go outside, I'll stay here."

A HOLDING ENVIRONMENT STRONG ENOUGH FOR JAMES

When I observed James, I didn't see a child suffering from a neurologic disorder such as emotionally disturbed. His lack of regard for others, his refusal to take direction, his lack of self-regulation and his angry and agitated demeanor all pointed to a child who was still looking out at the world from the perspective of omnipotence. What James needed was a holding environment that was strong enough to help him transition out of omnipotence and into interdependence.

A key element to creating an effective holding environment for James was to train his behaviorist to shift from giving information responses to inappropriate behavior, to giving short, regular time-outs (action responses). These would be supported by a consistent set of predictable, unyielding consequences that occurred if James refused to the follow direction to take a time out.

The basic tool of the behavior plan was to give James short, immediate time-outs on the spot. These were to be done without explaining to James what he'd done wrong. For instance, if he threw blocks, his behaviorist would tell him, "James, I need you to sit for sixty seconds right here." He would direct James to sit down a few feet away form the activity, quietly, for sixty seconds. The reason you don't tell him why is threefold. First, telling him why invites argument, manipulation and discussion, all of which can be stimulating and reinforcing. Second, when you discuss why you assume a certain malignant intention in the action being addressed when it might simply have been impulsive. Third, when you give the consequence without explanation you are letting the child know that your expectation is that he can figure out the reasons for the consequences and is expected to figure out those things that are common sense and considerate of others.

Initially, James would not take the direction from his behaviorist to sit quietly for one minute. He tried to run away, or negotiate his way out of taking the time out. Sometimes when his behaviorist caught him he would hit, kick, bite and spit in an attempt to get loose again. But the behaviorist followed a very predictable behavior protocol. If James didn't sit down within five seconds of being told, the consequence shifted to two minutes. If the behaviorist had to physically bring him to the time out spot, the consequences shifted to five minutes. If James wouldn't sit quietly on his own and needed to be held, the behaviorist held him firmly and silently until James had stopped struggling and was quiet and then he required James to sit quietly for five minutes while he held him loosely and five minutes quietly on his own.

During the first couple of days using the above protocol James never took the one-minute time out. He tested the limits and consistency of the protocol and needed to be held an average of four or five times a day. But gradually he adjusted to the protocol, each day showing an improved ability to exercise self-regulation. After two weeks he was taking the one-minute time outs regularly throughout the day and only needed to be held about once or twice a day and for much shorter time periods.

James's behaviorist Wayne now uses this simple tool to great effect. For instance: James is writing his letters at a table while talking to the classroom aide.

James says to the woman, "You're crazy. I'm going to call you *Crazy*."

"Don't call me Crazy. My name is Tracy. You can call me Miss Tracy."

James, "Okay, I'll call you Tracy."

"No, it's *Miss* Tracy,"

James smirked at her and said, "Okay, Tracy."

At this point Wayne said, "James, have a seat" and pointed to the floor one foot behind his chair. James got up and sat down on the spot.

After about a minute Wayne said, "Okay, James sit back in your chair." James understood why he'd been asked to have a seat on the floor for a minute and gave no objection.

Throughout the morning at pre-K, James' behaviorist gives him regular one-minute time outs on the spot. Because he gives them regularly and before James' behavior gets too severe, there is no need for missing recess or other consequences. Occasionally, if James looked as though he didn't understand why he'd been given a time out Wayne would ask him, "Do you know why I asked you to sit down?" Most of the time James would figure it out after thinking about it for a moment or after Wayne would ask him a follow-up question like, "If someone else has taken a toy out are we allowed to take it from their desk without asking them?" Giving James a chance to figure it out on his own or with the help of some leading questions provided an opportunity for Wayne to praise James for figuring it out. James might say, "Because I took the

Lego from Jimmy's desk?" and Wayne would smile and say, "Exactly," put his hand on James's shoulder and add, "So go back and play now."

Five months into the behavior program and James was a very different child. He was still impulsive and had a hard time controlling his hands and his mouth but gone were the angry oppositional behaviors, the violent behaviors and the refusal to take directions from adults. It was a great relief for James not to hear the constant, specific reminders of what he'd done wrong. So a switch from using information prompts like, "James, stop talking," "James, keep your hands to yourself," and "James, I told you twice already you need to get started," to simple action consequences such as, "James, have a seat," was a welcome relief.

When adults establish a strong holding environment using clear, predictable action consequences that cannot be manipulated, children can release the responsibility that accompanies their feelings of omnipotence. Once it was clear that the adults, not James, were in charge of things, he was able to move into the safer identity of interdependence and was free to be a child again.

The principle of giving regular, short, immediate consequences so as to gradually develop the psychological muscles of self-regulation works for both younger children and for older children who still lack the skills, or motivation, for self-regulation.

How Can I Stop the Cursing?

At a school for difficult children a teacher who taught eleven- and twelve-year olds, Mr. Davis, asked me if I could come to his class and give him some advice on cleaning up the foul language his students used. The problem was particularly difficult during recess when the boys were playing basketball.

If they missed a shot, "F**k!" If the other team scored, "G-d damn!" If a teammate made a mistake, "What the f**k!" They'd curse at the other team to try to get them riled and often tempers would get out of control and a staff would have to break it up.

Mr. Davis would stand on the sidelines telling them to tone it down, "David, stop cursing," "Alex, watch your mouth!" or "Ryan, if you keep cursing I'm gonna pull you out!" When he'd had enough he'd tell a student he was out of the game. But this usually resulted in a big argument, "Why am I out? Ryan was cursing too. What the f**k! This isn't fair. S**t."

Mr. Davis even tried benching everyone for a day, "That's it! Basketball's over for today. Find something else to do." But a day or two later the cursing was back in full swing. Mr. Davis felt constantly frustrated and boys seemed to sense exactly how much cursing they could get away with and when they'd see Mr. Davis was about to blow they'd pull it back or apologize and swear to Mr. Davis they'd stop.

I suggested that Mr. Davis use immediate one-minute time outs every time someone cursed, and to encourage compliance he should increase the time if they argued, refused or continued to curse. I talked about the importance of 100% follow-through and setting a strong precedent the first day he used the approach. We talked through the details and the best language to use and on the day he started I stood at the edge of the court to watch how it went.

Two minutes into the basketball game the cursing started. Mr. Davis stepped onto the court and said, "Everybody freeze!" The boys looked a bit puzzled. "Ryan, give me the ball." Ryan gave him the ball and Mr. Davis said, "I need you to have a seat for one minute." "Why? What'd I do?" Mr. Davis said to everyone, "Every time you curse you'll get a one-minute penalty." Ryan threw up his hands and said, "What the fu**k!" and Mr. Davis responded with, "Now you've got two minutes," and tossed the ball to Ryan's teammate and said, "Enjoy the game."

After two minutes he sent Ryan back in and a minute after that he benched Tony for a minute. During the next thirty minutes he gave out sixteen minutes in one-minute cursing penalties. The boys were visibly frustrated by the constant benching; at one point three of the eight boys playing were sitting down, but Mr. Davis was clearly less frustrated. When they'd get upset he'd coach them through the consequence, "Easy… it's just sixty seconds. Don't worry about it. You sit for a minute then go back and play." By the end of the game the boys were starting to tell each other to stop cursing, "Tony, thanks a lot! How we supposed to win with two of you on the bench?" The next day Mr. Davis only needed to give six one-minute penalties and by the end of the week it was down to three.

I checked in with Mr. Davis about a month later and he told me that he still needed to give an average of two or three cursing penalties per game but he felt like now he had a firm handle on the situation. The immediate one-minute cursing penalty shifted the frustration and responsibility to control the cursing off the shoulders of Mr. Davis and onto the shoulders of the boys doing the cursing. By switching from responding with information (telling them what they already know) to responding with action, the situation quickly turned around. This small, regular consequence was sufficient to motivate the boys to exercise enough restraint to seriously reduce the cursing.

LONG-TERM CONSEQUENCES DISCOURAGE FOR A LONG TIME

When managing behavior or setting up specific behavior protocols for children with problem behaviors, it is important to set up systems that allow the children to start again very often. Long-term rewards and consequences (like offering children a special pizza party at the end of the week/month for good behavior) is setting either them, or you, up for failure. There are only two ways a long-term consequence like this can go, and both ways are bad.

First, I often see a reward like this set up and then the teacher is unable to bring herself to actually deny the party to those who have not behaved. This usually entails a lot of second chances, apologies and negotiation to improve or never do it again. The end result is that the students learn that the teacher's contingent "if you're good" is empty and they will get the party no matter how they behave.

The second way this goes is the teacher does follow through with denying the party to either everyone or to those who haven't behaved. In this case the big motivator (pizza party) becomes the big discourager when someone has a rough day early in the week/month and feels discouraged from then on. Ronald has a "bad" day and the teacher tells him he won't be allowed to go to the pizza party so for the following eight days between that "bad" day and the pizza party Ronald is bitter, angry and unmotivated.

A lot of consequences that are given in the classroom are delayed, not immediate, consequences. For instance, a teacher might give "minutes" that are to be served later during recess. Each time a student is disruptive or inappropriate the teacher will give her time she owes: "You owe me five minutes of your recess." Sometimes the consequence comes in one big chunk as in, "That's it, Madison. You're benched for recess." Rather than motivating more self control, these types of consequences often de-motivate the child for the period of time between getting the consequence and when she actually has to receive it.

Additionally, I dislike the use of big, long-term consequences because it impairs the ability of the child to quickly regroup after difficulties and begin to make new choices from that moment on. I like to teach children that they have more control over the consequences of their actions than that. I've been in classrooms where very belligerent children have lost all their recess time for the next month. (This was due to their unwillingness to do class work so often that the accumulated make-up work to be done at recess would take a month of recesses to complete.)

Behavior programs should be set up so as to allow children to change the direction of things at any time. In the worst-case scenario the consequence of the child's accumulated choices might result in one bad day. The next day she should be able to start fresh.

Chapter 8

Coaching Lions

FROM OPPONENT TO COACH

Our first reaction when someone tries to move us is to oppose him. When we try to move someone in one direction, he naturally pushes in the opposite one. Children are no different; when children feel like you are trying to make them do something, manipulate them, or influence their decision, their first reaction will likely be to resist you, and even the more so during moments of conflict or with children with skewed feelings of their own power or omnipotence.

Although the last thing most parents and teachers want is an adversarial relationship with their children and students, this is exactly what develops when they attempt to set boundaries, enforce rules or offer well-meaning advice. So the question becomes how we can effectively shift our relationships with our children during moments of conflict or difficulty from one of opponent to one of coach.

SOOTHING THE IMPULSES OF OMNIPOTENCE

Children with a strong omnipotent identity are keenly aware of their own power; they feel entitled to choices and autonomy; they are more aware of the subtleties of communication; and they aggressively assert their will. While the majority of today's children share these characteristics and qualities, those with severe behavior problems have the more extreme version of these characteristics. Therefore, the kind of language that is effective with children with strong omnipotent identities is also very effective with all of today's children.

Effectively communicating with today's children, especially when their will and yours are in conflict, requires that you verbally recognize their autonomy, power and ability while simultaneously asserting your own.

The following are the basic rules found in the language of the Meet the Hand approach:

1. ***Acknowledge their power*** *– let the child know you recognize that she, not you, makes her choices.*

2. ***Use the language of choice*** *– talk about the decisions and the consequences of those decisions in terms of choices to be made by the child.*

3. ***Don't let it get personal*** *– remove your own emotional judgment or offense from your child's bad decisions and your administering of consequences.*

4. ***Shift from opponent to coach*** *– when the child blames you, affirm you want the child to be able to get what she wants, and reframe the consequences as the natural order of things.*

5. ***Never moralize to them*** *– children recognize moralizing for what it is—manipulation—and the use of it encourages an oppositional response and will undermine your recognition of their autonomy.*

6. ***Always, no matter what, do what you say you'll do 100% of the time*** *– when adults use predictable and reasonable boundaries, children stop fighting so vigorously against them, because adults are more trusted and the child's world feels safer and more in control.*

VERBAL JUJITSU

While it is important to set and hold firm boundaries and consequences in the home and classroom, it is not necessary to do so in an
adversarial or oppositional manner. In fact, it is more difficult, not to
mention a lot less fun, to use an oppositional approach than a coaching
one. The key to shifting the dynamic is to use a set of communication
tools and mindsets that, collectively, I call *Verbal Jujitsu*.

Shift your approach to conflict dynamics so you can give the child
what she needs while firmly asserting what you need. At first the omnipotent identity child will be accustomed to asserting her own will while
negating yours, and it will be up to you as the adult to frame the consequences and communication in such a way that holds in balance both
the recognition of the child and the adult's needs. If the adult attempts to
hold the boundary or consequence with the child in a way that negates
the child's needs, then the child will continue to perceive the adult as her
opposition and not her coach.

You can imagine the oppositional dynamic as looking like this:

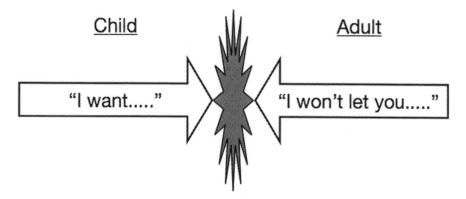

The adult and the child are on two opposing sides.

AND VERBAL JUJITSU LOOKING LIKE THIS:

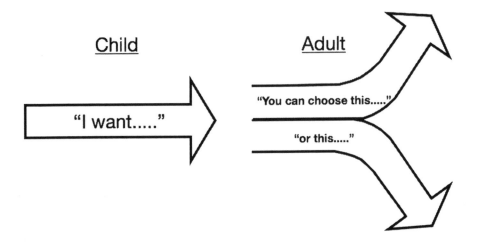

Verbal Jujitsu starts with the mindset that each action has its natural consequence and, as the adult, your job is to explain and administer these consequences. Teach them that the world works by the rules of cause and effect. These rules naturally benefit those who take actions that go with these rules and naturally frustrate those who go against them. It isn't necessary for adults to get angry or judgmental because any poor decisions (causes) will have their own accompanying frustrations (effects).

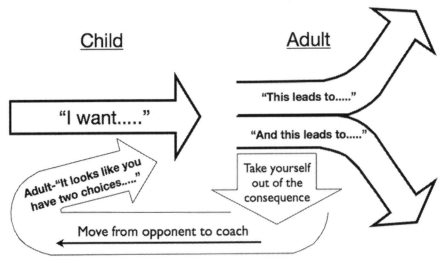

Verbal Jujitsu also allows the adult to shift his relationship with the child from one of opposing her to working alongside her.

Depersonalize problems and boundaries and move to the side of your child:

Imagine yourself standing next to your child while you both look toward the choice/consequence she is facing.

GRACE AND REBECCA

In the anecdote that follows, I use the techniques of Verbal Jujitsu to effectively enforce the classroom rules.

Everything about Grace seemed round. She looked as though she'd been put together with balls of dough. Even her hair was in perfectly round curls. She was fourteen years old and developmentally delayed, but you'd never know it from the way she ran the school staff ragged. Grace was always wandering around the school with a teacher's aide following her. As much as the staff tried to teach, direct and contain her, Grace was constantly finding some way to do only those things she wanted to do, and that was often wandering the halls socializing instead of being in class. When the staff did set firm limits, Grace would refuse to listen, run away from or hit the staff, or lie on the floor and refuse to move. She had a little crush on the guy who ran the time-out room at the end of the hall, so sending her there wasn't an effective consequence. Grace was usually carrying around her doll, Rebecca, and would often insist she have it with her or she needed to go and get it. Sometimes Grace would decide she needed to sleep and would lie down on the floor in the middle of class with a pillow. Because she was taking a number of strong medications in an attempt to control her behavior, it was difficult to know whether her need to sleep in class was legitimate or a manipulation.

We set up a detailed behavior plan for Grace and trained all the staff who worked with her to use it in exactly the same way. One of the rules of the class under the behavior plan was that if Grace needed to sleep then she could leave the room and we'd find her a quiet place to sleep. But there was no sleeping in the classroom. Additionally, Grace could only keep her doll Rebecca with her when she was in the classroom. If she needed to leave the classroom Rebecca stayed in the class until she got back. This rule was also set up to increase Grace's motivation to stay in class.

At about 10:30 a.m. on the first day of the new behavior plan, Grace got up during the middle of the math lesson and announced, "I'm taking a nap." She got a pillow off the shelf and began to lie down on the floor in front of her teacher as he was teaching.

Grace's behaviorist Laura and I got to Grace as she began to lie down and said, "Grace, if you want to sleep, then you need to leave the class to sleep. There's no sleeping in class."

Grace whined and said, "Leave me alone, I need to sleep," and tried to push us away.

But Laura and I were persistent and as I lifted Grace's pillow off the ground, Laura held Grace's arm, sat her up, and said, "If you need to sleep, then you can sleep, Grace. You just need to leave the class and sleep somewhere else" (*Language of Choice*).

Grace continued to resist us for another minute or so, "I hate you! Leave me alone, I'm tired I want to sleep."

Laura and I kept repeating to Grace that it was okay to sleep, she just needed to leave the room to do it. (*Acknowledge their power* – **We can't/won't stop her from sleeping**).

After almost a minute of this, Grace got up and started walking with us to the door. Then she decided she needed Rebecca and grabbed her off the desk.

We waited until Grace was just outside the classroom door, then we stopped her and said, "Grace, Rebecca needs to stay in the classroom."

Grace whined loudly, "You can't take Rebecca away! I want to stay with Rebecca."

Laura said to her, "I don't want to take Rebecca. I'd love you to stay with Rebecca but the rules are Rebecca always stays in the class." (*Stay on their side* and *don't let it get personal*)

"But I want Rebecca!" said Grace.

I said to her, "Grace, you can stay with Rebecca but then you need to stay in class and there's no sleeping in class." (*Language of Choice*)

"But I need to go to sleep. Why won't you let me go to sleep?" said Grace.

"If you want to go to sleep, that's okay, we'll take you to a quiet room where you can sleep."

Laura and I went back and forth like this with Grace. Each time she'd insist she wanted to sleep we'd agree and tell her she could sleep or we'd tell her she didn't have to give up Rebecca if she stayed in the class. After a minute or two Grace gave up arguing with us and stood thinking for a moment. Then she said, "I'm going to stay with Rebecca" and walked back into class. As she did we insisted she give us the pillow under her arm, which she did. Grace stayed in class until lunchtime without a nap.

After about a week we knew that Grace's need to sleep during the middle of class was in large part a manipulation or an attempt to get attention. There was only one time during that week when Grace took us up on the offer to let her sleep in another room. When we did put her in a quiet little room to sleep she lay down for less than a minute then decided she didn't need it and went back to class. After this Grace never again tried to sleep in class.

The rules about no sleeping in class, and Rebecca needs to stay in class, can be seen as the firm hand meeting the child's hand. The emphasizing of Grace's choices that allow her to determine the outcome of the situation effectively reinforced her sense of power and independence. Finally, the neutral, nonjudgmental way in which Laura and I explained how things worked shifted the tone from oppositional to coaching and greased the wheels for Grace to make a decision that was based in interdependence and not omnipotence.

In the above interaction, the acknowledging of her power happens through the continual shift from conflict to choice. Sometimes the need to acknowledge a child's power is even more acute.

GIVE THEM WHAT THEY NEED

Children who have strong feelings of omnipotence, whether from neglect or from care, crave not only strong boundaries but also a clear acknowledging of their independence. If you attempt to assert strong boundaries without simultaneously using language that recognizes their independence and power, the omnipotent child will resist you longer and more forcefully than he would otherwise.

When we attempt to set firm boundaries without recognizing the child's independence and power, we are essentially asking the child to recognize our power while denying his own. This is unnecessary and counterproductive; it's asking for a fight that we don't need to have.

When we set firm boundaries while recognizing the power and independence of the child, we are asking the child to recognize our power while we recognize his. This is a respectful interaction and the child will grow from it into a person with a healthy capacity for mutual recognition.

If I'm working with a child with a very strong sense of omnipotence, recognizing the child's independence and power are not simply helpful but necessary if I'm going to turn him around. It's the difference between trying to force him into a room with no way out or blocking the entrance to certain rooms while allowing him to choose entrance into others.

Given the scenario below, the omnipotent child will almost always choose to fight you.

In the above scenario, fighting against the adult is a safer option than submitting. Because submitting means giving up the independence the child is trying to establish and the power he asserts to feel safe. If the omnipotent child does submit to you in the above scenario, he will do so with bitterness, and the capacity for intimacy and mutual recognition is undermined; and, the child will fight you the next time just as hard or harder.

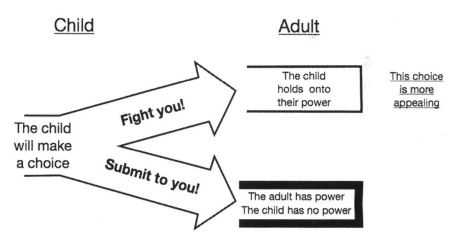

In the scenario below, the omnipotent child is given a way to recognize you and keep his dignity. So he is more likely to recognize you and the boundary you've set.

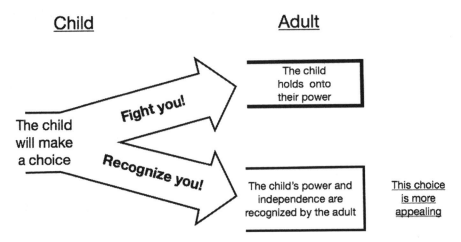

In this scenario the omnipotent child will most likely still fight you, but the fight will not last as long or be as ferocious. Because while he must give up the power to control and negate you, he can do so in a relationship that gives him the recognition of his independence and power he craves. Furthermore, because this is a scenario that gives him what he needs (but not what he wants), it builds intimacy and respect and the child is more likely to acknowledge you and the boundary you set in the future.

Instead of:
"You need to do what I say"

Try:
"You need to make a decision"

Who's the Boss?

One day I was walking down the hall at a school where I work regularly and saw the time-out staff, Alex, with a seven-year-old named Thomas. Thomas's hands were clenched into fists on the side of his body and he was red-faced, with tears streaming down his cheeks, screaming,

"YOU'RE NOT THE BOSS OF ME! YOU'RE NOT THE BOSS OF ME!"

Alex, looked tired and a little frustrated as he tried to get through to Thomas, "Look, Thomas, you've got to listen to me! If you don't come into the time-out room, I'm going to take you to isolation."

"YOU'RE NOT THE BOSS OF ME!" Thomas yelled back.

"Thomas, you've got to stop saying that. You've got to do what I say."

Still crying and screaming, Thomas repeated, "YOU'RE NOT THE BOSS OF ME! YOU'RE NOT THE BOSS OF ME!"

Alex saw me and said "Joe, can you do something with this kid? He just keeps telling me I'm not the boss of him. He's got to learn to follow my directions."

"Well, I can try," I said.

I stepped up to Thomas and immediately he shouted at me, "YOU'RE NOT THE BOSS OF ME! YOU'RE NOT THE BOSS OF ME!"

I put my hands up to indicate "I surrender" and said, "You're right. I *am not* the boss of you."

Thomas screamed it again, "YOU'RE NOT THE BOSS OF ME!" with tears still streaming down both cheeks.

"That's right. I am definitely *not* the boss of you, Thomas. You are the boss of you."

Still crying, he got a little quieter and said again, "You're not the boss of me."

I repeated it again, "I am not the boss of you" then after a pause I said, "But you've got a decision to make. You can calm down and come into the time-out room, or if you're standing in the hall screaming and crying, you have to go to isolation. Do you want to go to isolation?"

To my surprise he said, "Yes!"

I said, "Okay, come on." At which point he took my hand and we walked quietly to the isolation room together.

Children have power and it's important to recognize it. When a child is being oppositional and defiant, sometimes the first step to defusing the situation is to acknowledge his power. Children with strong feelings of omnipotence cling to their perceived power because it's their safety line to keeping control of a scary world. The language I use when dealing with an oppositional situation, whether it's eight-year-old Thomas or my seventeen-year-old stepdaughter, is always more effective when I acknowledge the power of the person I'm dealing with. Once you've clearly acknowledged the power of the other, it becomes much easier to clearly set boundaries.

The truth is, I'm not the boss of Thomas. I think we get into trouble when we think we can make kids do what they don't want to do. When I do staff trainings I like to tell them, "You are not in charge of behavior. The children are in charge of behavior. You are in charge of consequences. If you don't like the behavior, change the consequences." In the end teachers and parents are really only in charge of motivation. If a child doesn't want to do something he isn't going to do it, unless you make it in his best interest.

DON'T HOLD WHAT'S THEIRS

In addition to Verbal Jujitsu being a very effective means of dealing with conflict, it also communicates to the child in a way that supports the kind of healthy thinking we want him to develop and use.

Most children with behavior problems have developed a pattern of externalizing their problems and difficulties. Whatever goes wrong is blamed on the adults around them. Remember that while externalizing is a natural and healthy survival tool for an infant, a child should shift from externalizing to internalizing many difficulties as he moves into interdependence.

GUIDANCE WITHOUT MANIPULATION

There are all kinds of subtle manipulations in the language we use when we talk with children. This new generation of children, children with stronger omnipotent identities and stronger sense of themselves, are highly sensitive to manipulation and they will resist it. The use of manipulation is an attempt to shape and change them based in a fear that the child will not come to the correct conclusions on his own. The child's resistance will start an antagonistic and oppositional dynamic. The most effective way to speak to these children is to speak to them in terms that acknowledge their independent will.

Recognize that children ultimately make the decisions in each circumstance and that we cannot make decisions for them. Also, the language that we use with children should communicate to them a belief that they are capable of making logical, healthy decisions that are respectful of themselves and others. The language commonly used to speak with children is filled with manipulation, moralizing and innuendo about what they should and shouldn't do. This kind of language communicates to them our lack of faith in both their ability to make decisions, and in their capacity as moral and ethical persons.

LEARNING OR REALIZATION?

There are two different ways to teach a child: through a process of learning or a process of realization. When you're trying to teach a child after a moment of conflict or difficulty, it is much more effective to use a process of realization.

Learning happens when you take information, or the conclusion about something, from someone else. The adult gives the information or conclusion and the child takes it.

Realization happens when you gather your own information and come to the conclusion on your own. The adult can lead a child to realizations by asking questions rather than giving answers.

Using a series of questions to lead someone to certain realizations is commonly called the Socratic method. Wikipedia defines Socratic method as "a form of philosophical inquiry in which the questioner explores the implications of others' positions, to stimulate rational thinking and illuminate ideas."

JIMMY'S ONE FRIEND

One afternoon, I was watching Jimmy ("I hate polite children", chapter 6) playing Legos with two other boys when I heard him say to his friend Ryan, "That's a stupid way to build it. The wings are gonna fall off. Give me the ship, you're stupid."

Ryan looked hurt, put the half-built spaceship down and turned his back to Jimmy.

Jimmy was in the first grade now and had come a long way from where he'd started. But he was still very impulsive and often said the first thing that popped into his mind without thinking. He was trying his best to make friends but most of the children still didn't like him very much. He and Ryan had become friends about two months earlier and had even had a few play dates together after school.

I winced when I heard him call Ryan stupid, not only because he clearly hurt Ryan's feelings, but also because I was afraid he might lose one of his precious few friends. So I called Jimmy over and said to him, "Jimmy, let me ask you a question. Do you want to have more friends?"

Jimmy looked at me suspiciously and gave a tentative, "Yes."

"Okay, and are you happy about how many play dates you have or do you want to have more?"

"I want to have more." Jimmy said.

"So right now, after what you just said to him, do you think Ryan wants to be your friend?"

"But Ryan was being stupid. If you put the wings on like that they'll never stay. You need to ..."

I broke in and said, "Hold on, hold on. I didn't ask you if Ryan was being stupid, maybe he was. I'm just asking you if you think he wants to be your friend when you call him stupid."

"I don't know. Probably not," he said.

"Well I just wanted to ask you because I know you want to have more friends and play dates, so I couldn't figure out why you called Ryan stupid."

Then after a pause I said, "Do you want to go back and play?"

"Yeah." Jimmy said.

"Go on then."

Jimmy had always been resistant to anyone telling him that something he did was wrong or a bad idea. I'd learned that if I asked him questions, and didn't force him to admit he was wrong, he was more likely to talk with me honestly and change his behavior.

DID THAT WORK FOR YOU?

The key to having a Socratic dialogue with children is to base your discussion around asking them, in as many ways as possible, **"Did the choices you made get you what you wanted?"**

When you lead a child to examine the facts and ideas based on better understanding what's in her own self-interest, rather than telling her your conclusions about what she should and shouldn't do, she will more easily embrace the realizations and conclusions she's come to because she feels respected and not manipulated.

In order for a Socratic dialogue to take place, there must be some problem, dilemma or frustration to be eliminated. Problems lead to frustrations, which lead to questions, which lead to answers.

Sometimes you need to create the frustration to get things started, like when I watched five-year-old James rush through writing his letters for homework. I saw him writing letters so fast they were barely legible and far from his best work.

When James gave me the first page, I told him, " I'm sorry, I can't read this. You'll need to do it again." He took the page back, erased what he'd written, and wrote the letters again at top speed.

When he brought it to me this time I said, "Well, these first few letters look good, but the rest look the same as before. You're going to have erase all these and do them again." Then I added, "Let me ask you a question: Why do you think these look so messy?"

"Well I did them real fast. So I can go play," he said.

"Okay, well erase these and do them again so they are neat."

James went back to the desk, erased the messy ones, and again wrote them illegibly at top speed.

When he brought me his paper I looked at it and said, "Wow, it kind of looks the same. These first ones look good then it looks real messy. What did you do on these first ones that look real neat?"

"I did those real slow," he answered.

"Well, how come you don't do the rest that way so you don't have to erase them?" I asked.

"If I go slow it takes too long and I want to finish so I can go play," he responded.

"Let me ask you a question. What do you think will take longer—doing this page fast *but doing it five times*, or doing this page slow *but just doing it once*?" I asked.

He looked at me with a half smile and said, "Probably, doing it one time slow."

"So your theory is that it would be faster to do the letters one time but slow? Well if that's your theory, maybe you should test that out," I suggested.

THE CHILD MUST HAVE A QUESTION

The general question you want your child to come to is, "What must I do to alleviate this frustration?" Without this initial question there is no motivation (fuel) for realization. To get the thinking started, ask questions that require reflection. First ask general questions, then get more specific, but never give more information than necessary.

General question – "What do you think you could do to make this more legible?"

More Specific – "When you wrote this did you go fast, medium or slow? Which way do you think would produce the best-looking letters?"

A child who comes from a system of interaction that allowed her omnipotence to remain dominant will associate safety with keeping control over things. This manifests as a need to be perfect and a resistance to anyone telling her what to do. So when an adult tells her what she is doing wrong, or what she should be doing that she is not, she is naturally resistant. Taking information from others (learning) feels unsafe or out-of-control, whereas coming to new conclusions on her own reinforces her need to feel her independence.

I used to run a mentoring program for children ages seven to twelve. Once a week the adult mentors led a philosophical discussion with the children about various social, moral and ethical issues. We had a very strict rule that the adults in the room, including the moderator of the discussion, could only ask questions; never give answers or opinions. These discussions were wildly successful. They forced the adults to think deeply about what they wanted to communicate and it created an atmosphere of structured respect and freedom where the children owned the conversation and felt at ease to speak their minds.

When an adult is giving a child information and conclusions about her behaviors, they are denying the child the opportunity to gather information and reach conclusions on her own. When you lead a child to reach conclusions on her own, the child will be more likely to remember and use those conclusions because they are paired with the feelings of accomplishment at having figured it out herself.

Chapter 9

The Lion's Pride

In the home or in the classroom, behavior methods and programs are only effective when they are done consistently and fit together in a manner so that one action supports the other.

There are many well-trained and skilled professionals working in public and special needs schools. These teachers, aides, therapists and specialists are trained in a manner that gives them an assortment of different skills and tools to use as they see fit. But which skills and tools they use vary from person to person and from moment to moment. This means there is an array of loopholes and contradicting motivators that are easily manipulated by children with powerful capacities to control those around them.

For instance, the consequence for acting out in class may be to be sent out of the room to a time-out room. But when the child gets to the time-out room, the staff there talks with her until the child is ready to return. While some children come into the time-out room upset and the staff's talk with them is effective in temporarily calming them down, other children come to the time-out room because talking with the staff there is more interesting than participating in the history lesson. In either case, the root problem is not treated.

Real solutions for children with very difficult behaviors requires detailed protocols that clearly define the specific consequences, language and the role of every staff that interacts with a particular child. I call these programs **Therapeutic Interaction Systems** (T.I.S.).

While the T.I.S. programs that follow mostly focus on children with more extreme behaviors, the principles found in them apply to every parent who wants to raise healthier, better-behaved children. Remember, if your child receives more stimulation from your solving of their tantrum than they do from not having one in the first place you might end that particular tantrum but you'll set yourself up for many more.

THERAPEUTIC INTERACTION SYSTEM

A Therapeutic Interaction System creates the environment needed to allow the child to transition from omnipotence to interdependence.

In chapter 7 I describe how a mother used short action consequences to teach her three-year-old daughter Sophie how to develop the self-regulation needed to participate in dance class. When we look at the consequences the mother used in that scenario we can see the beginnings of a Therapeutic Interaction System.

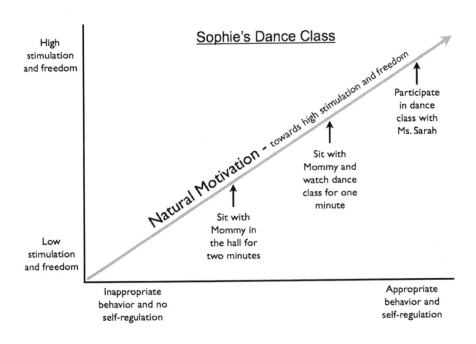

Sophie's mother used the stages above in a way that allowed Sophie to move easily from one stage to another based on her short exertions and reasonable amounts of self-control. Sophie was thus motivated to try and control herself so that she could get the stimulation she enjoyed from the dance class. Additionally, getting what she wanted quickly within the boundaries reinforced her efforts at self-control. Furthermore, she was able to exercise her muscles of self-control a little at a time over and over again to gradually make them stronger.

Before using the above method, Sophie's mother would tell her over and over again that she needed to behave and finally when she'd had enough she would take her home early (the "straw that broke the camel's back" method from the beginning of chapter 7). Sophie had very few opportunities to regroup and come back into the class. Instead of learning to gradually exercise self-control she was learning that she couldn't cope with the requirements of dance class.

As children with strong omnipotent identities get older and enter school, the challenge of creating effective, consistent boundaries becomes more complicated. One of the biggest challenges is coordinating the efforts of the many different adults the children will interact with at school. Even schools that specialize in working with behavior problem children rarely have staff that have been trained to work in a choreographed and synchronized way. Consequently, children who have highly developed abilities to manipulate and act out find plenty of loopholes and inconsistencies to take advantage of. Each time an omnipotent child successfully manipulates or avoids a consequence or boundary, her sense of her own omnipotence grows stronger.

For behavior specialists at public schools and for staff at schools for children with behavior problems, the goal is often to calm children down (de-escalate them) and get them back in class. The goal of a

Therapeutic Interaction System is not to calm children down, but to teach them to calm themselves.

For staff to simply try to calm a child down and get her back to class is for them to attack the effect of the child's problem and not its cause. The cause of the child's inability to control herself is omnipotence. Therefore, the goal of a Therapeutic Intervention System is to create an environment and interactions (sometimes called a "holding environment") that enable the child to transition out of omnipotence and into interdependence.

Essentially the problems developed because the child's environment wasn't strong enough to contain the omnipotent identity and develop the healthy tension of mutual recognition; consequently, the child did not develop the muscles and habits of self-regulation. A T.I.S. program is the extra strong holding environment necessary to contain a child with a super strong sense of omnipotence.

A T.I.S. is a program that unifies all the adults that interact with a child at a school so that they become, in effect, of a kind of super-parent whose actions and language are tailored to provide a strong, consistent and sophisticated system that can consistently hold strong boundaries while using language that helps the child transition into interdependence.

The T.I.S. program for eight-year-old Emma, who'd been diagnosed as bipolar because of her escalating rages, tantrums and manipulations, included detailed steps of predictable consequences as well as specific language to be used by staff in response to all problem behaviors.

When consequences in a behavior plan don't fit together in a coherent system they don't work. For instance, I'll go into a classroom and see a teacher give a time-out to a disruptive student but the time-out desk has books to read that are more interesting than the lesson being taught. If the student becomes really disruptive the teacher sends him out of the room to the crisis room down the hall. The student likes the staff in the crisis room and finds them interesting. They will talk with him in an effort to calm him down so he can be sent back to class. If the student becomes physically aggressive, the school staff may physically restrain the student or put him in an isolation room and then call the student's counselor who will bring the student back to their office where they will talk and perhaps play a board game.

The graph below shows the system of actions and consequences in the setting above:

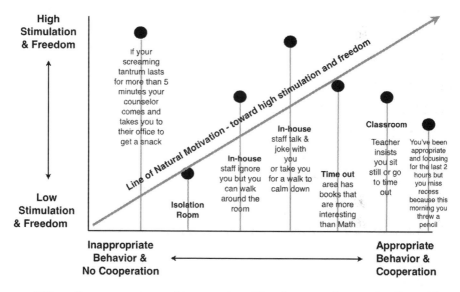

When I see a system of interaction like the one above, the first thing I ask myself is, "How can I shift things to make classroom participation more interesting and rewarding and make inappropriate behavior less interesting and rewarding?" The goal is to make appropriate behavior and classroom participation the most rewarding choice for the student. I want all the consequences of the student's choices to fall along that diagonal line that motivates appropriate behavior.

To do this I need to do two things. First, adjust the consequences so that they fall on that diagonal line. Second, make sure that each person in that setting consistently administers those consequences the same way.

The first thing I do to adjust the consequences is to take away ineffective or counterproductive consequences in the classroom to make the classroom a more desirable place for the student:

- We change the consequences in the class to make them immediate and short in duration. No more missing twenty minutes of recess because of behavior that occurred two hours before.

- Next we eliminate consequences for impulsive behaviors that are not disruptive. It's okay for the student to stand or pace behind his desk so long as he is attentive and working.

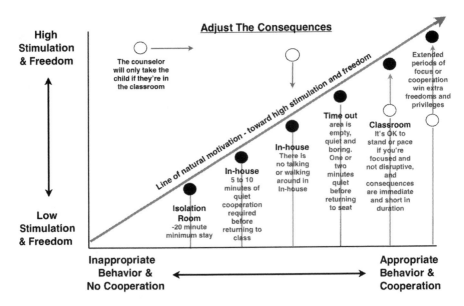

After I've made the classroom more appealing, I work to make the consequences progressively less appealing:

- Make sure there is nothing to do at the focus desk in the classroom.

- The staff in the crisis room refuse to have any conversation with students who are there.
- Students in the crisis room must stand or sit in one place until they have finished the tasks required to return to class.
- The counselors agree they will only take students from class and not from the crisis room. Making sure that students aren't being rewarded for actions that resulted in them having to leave the classroom.

Once you have a good behavior plan the next step is to make sure it's applied consistently. There are three areas to look at in order to make a behavior plan consistent:

- <u>Your own actions</u> - Stay consistent in your own application of the plan.
- <u>The actions of the various adults in a given setting</u> - Coordinate all those in the particular setting (home, classroom, dance class) to apply the plan in the same way (in some cases this might be just one person, you!)
- <u>The actions of the adults in each different setting</u> - *If you can*, coordinate the adults in the child's different settings to do the same plan. If this isn't possible (like in the case of a child who's being raised in two different homes with parents who don't agree on one method, or a home and school where one party isn't onboard with the plan) then make sure the consequences of the behavior plan don't require the cooperation of anyone outside of the setting in which you have buy in.

Most of the behavior interventions I've done in the last eighteen years *didn't* have all three levels of consistency outlined above.

Particularly in the earlier years of doing my method the only thing that I could guarantee was the consistency of my own actions, so I made great effort to make sure I was the one who gave consequences in the given setting (usually a classroom or school).

When I'm brought into a school to design behavior protocols for difficult students, one of the common questions I'm asked is, "Won't we need to get the parents doing the same thing in order for this to work?" Sometimes a divorced parent will ask the similar question, "Doesn't my ex need to be doing the same program if this is going to work at all?" The short answer to both of these questions is "No."

While it is always better for the child and easier for the adults if everyone is on the same page, it isn't necessary. I know this because of the many cases I've worked on where getting everyone on the same page and using the same approach was impossible. Sometimes the child's mother was caring for her son in a homeless shelter. Sometimes the two parents lived in separate homes and weren't talking. And in some cases the parents were unable to, or simply refused to, reflect on and shift the way they did things at home.

What I learned through all this was that children will adapt and respond differently to various environments. For instance a child might move through several distinct systems of interaction, each with its own rules and players. Molly's environments might include her mother's home, the elementary school, the soccer field, and her father's house. At her mother's house she may be completely out of control, while at school and on the soccer field she has very few problems, and at her father's house she is again very different. I've seen children who, a year into a successful behavior plan, are attentive and respectful with the adults at school but the same child will scream at and hit their mother when she arrives to pick them up from school.

180

Just go into any middle school or high school and follow a different student from one teacher to another and you'll see that the same children will behave, or misbehave, entirely differently with different teachers. Students who were loud, disruptive and rude to one teacher are often quiet, attentive and respectful ten minutes later in another class with another teacher.

Children learn and adapt to different environments, to different systems of interaction. In order to bring about a major change in a child's behavior, it isn't necessary to change all the systems of interaction she moves through, but rather to fix one of the environments so that it becomes one distinct system in which you can control most or all of the motivators and consequences.

Don't get me wrong: whenever possible, all the adults who interact with a child should get on the same page. Certainly the fastest and most thorough transformations I've seen have been with the children where that was the case. But when this isn't possible, a behavior plan that is a self-contained system will work wonders.

CONFLICTING MOTIVATORS

I often go to schools and see that the behavior plan as it's set up is full of holes and contradicting motivators. For instance, whenever eight-year-old William can't sit still and instead fiddles with something in his desk, the teacher's aide tells him, "William, if you don't get started I'm going to take away ten minutes of recess." But she says this ten to fifteen times before she actually takes it away. If the resource specialist sees he's having trouble focusing, she gives William a "sensory break," which means she takes him outside and lets him run around for five minutes to release his energy. Sometimes if the teacher sees he's unfocused, he's given chores to do in class.

The relationship between self-control and stimulation look like this:

- Exercise high self-control – Do the regular work assigned
  – Medium Stimulation
- Exercise less self-control – The threat of missing recess (1 in 10)
  – Low Stimulation
- Repeated lack of self-control – Go outside for five minutes (1 in 5)
  – High Stimulation
- Repeated lack of self-control – Do chores for the teacher (1 in 5)
  – High Stimulation

Because the consequences for his actions haven't been coordinated in a manner that consistently motivates self-control, William is motivated to repeatedly act out as much as he is to apply effort to his schoolwork.

The same set of consequences could be coordinated to motivate self-control by setting them up as follows.

- Exercise **very high self-control** - Finish work before the end of the period
  o Go outside for five minutes – **Highest stimulation**
- Exercise **high self-control** - Remained focused on class work for fifteen minutes
  o Do one chore for the teacher in class – **High Stimulation**
- Exercise **medium self-control** – Able to slowly move through class work
  o Remain at desk doing class work – **Medium Stimulation**
- Exercise **low self-control** – consistently unfocused and not doing his assignment

- o Sit at the focus desk for one minute with nothing to do – **Low Stimulation**
- Exercise **lowest self-control** – go to the focus desk so often that a minimum amount of class work isn't finished
    - Remain in class at recess until unfinished work is complete – **Lowest Stimulation**

A behavior plan that was structured like the one above would initially be set up tailored to fit the current abilities of a given student. If fifteen minutes of continued concentration on a task was entirely unheard of, then you would start at a level that was doable when motivated. As the child's abilities to focus and remain on task increased so would the times and tasks required to reach the goals built into the behavior plan.

MORE HOMEWORK, PLEASE?

Recently, I went into a school to troubleshoot a behavior protocol for a third-grader named Samantha. She had a basic protocol that gave her short time outs in the classroom when her behaviors became too inappropriate or manipulative. She wasn't allowed to bring her class work to the time outs, and if she fell behind with her work she needed to finish it before she went to snack, recess or lunch. The program was very successful until after lunchtime each day. Because there wasn't another break until school was over, Samantha would often refuse to work, indulge in back talk, and disrupt others every afternoon. Any work she didn't finished in the afternoon was sent home as homework. But Samantha didn't seem to mind this and would act out during any assignments she didn't like and didn't care how often she was given time outs. The work was sent home and always came back finished the next day.

With a little investigation I found out that Samantha's mother rewarded her nightly with toys and video games for doing her homework, and the more homework she did, the more video time and toys she got. Furthermore, her mother was easily fooled by Samantha's claim that the work was too difficult and would sit with her while she did it, often providing the answers. (The teacher refused to believe Samantha's claims of "It's too hard" and knew that, when pressed, she was capable of much more than she let on.) When tested on her work at school, Samantha was retaining very little of what she wasn't completing in the afternoon and took home as homework.

Behavior plans should be developed so that the causes and effects of each plan should be entirely contained within the school environment. I have never sent a child home with a consequence to be carried out by the parents or a note about how she misbehaved and shouldn't get certain privileges. First of all, I wanted the child to be able to start fresh when she left school. You never know how a consequence or reward will be given at home and whether it will support the style and rules of the program you've set up at the school.

While it would seem strange for a mother to drop her son off at school and tell the teacher he had misbehaved and should not be allowed to go to recess, it is common practice for a teacher or behaviorist to send a child home with a report about the child's misbehaving at school and request that she be punished or denied certain privileges. So when I develop a behavior plan, I make sure it's a self-contained plan.

"I Want Kung Fu Panda!"

Sometimes despite all your efforts to the contrary, a behavior plan that appears self-contained breaks down because of outside influences.

The Lion's Pride

I was working with a seven-year-old boy named Christopher who was mildly autistic and very oppositional. He would become fixated on consequences and would scream hysterically when he was given one. He was particularly oppositional when it came time to do any school-work that wasn't preferred and would throw books or pencils and would often hit the staff.

We'd set up a behavior plan that included activities that he enjoyed for five minutes at the end of every hour, short immediate consequences, and verbal prompts that redirected his attention away from negative consequences and onto working toward the activities he enjoyed. The program worked like a dream for about five weeks after which things started to break down. At this point he was becoming hysterical whenever he would be given a consequence for acting out or refusing to do class work. He would hit the staff, throw things and often have to be physically removed from the class to avoid him injuring others.

When I went in to observe him and to see if I could figure out what was going on, I noticed Christopher was again fixating on the negative consequences. He seemed to be reacting entirely out of proportion to the small consequences he was being given. When he would become hysterical he would also obsess about some upcoming movie he wanted to see, "No, I won't go to the focus desk! I want *Kung Fu Panda*!" On another occasion he yelled, "PLEASE don't take me to the time-out room! I'll be good! I have to have my Iron Man party!" We tried to console him by telling him he wasn't bad or in trouble, we wouldn't take away any party, and that when he'd calmed down he could come back to the classroom but this had no effect.

Finally, one day when he was in the time-out room he calmed himself, became very serious and said to me, "You don't understand. I can't be here. If I'm in the time-out room I don't get my Iron Man party."

Then he started to cry. At this point I realized what was fueling Christopher's fixation and seeming overreaction to the short consequences had to do with consequences and rewards he was getting at home.

Every day Christopher went home with a check sheet from the teacher that outlined how he had done and what had happened. Encouraged by the five weeks of progress he had made and eager to see it continue, his parents had decided to give him incentives for continuing the good work at school. They'd told him that if he didn't have to go to the focus desk in class or the time-out room down the hall, then they would give him special treats. One week it was taking him to see the movie *Kung Fu Panda*. Another time they promised they'd make him a special Iron Man-themed party if he did well for two straight weeks.

Set up with the best of intentions, the reward system at home had undermined the effectiveness of the program at school. The system of short, immediate, small consequences had become a system of big, long-term consequences. And because his parents weren't specific about what amount of problem behavior disqualified him for the rewards they'd set up, Christopher assumed any mistake could ruin everything. If he went to the focus desk on Monday, became hysterical and was taken to the time-out room, he might be unmotivated and discouraged every day for the next two weeks.

After a talk with his parents, explaining what we were seeing, they stopped setting up consequences and rewards for his behaviors at school. Within two weeks the behavior plan at school started working again.

This is an example of a behavior environment that sprung a leak and wasn't working because of outside consequences. The solution was to find the hole, patch it and reseal the behavior environment.

Conclusion

Mutual recognition, that internal tension between the needs of the self and the needs of others, is the basis for our children's healthy psychological development and must become the cornerstone of our approach to child rearing. Without it, our children become emotionally feeble, lonely, anxiety-ridden, undisciplined and narcissistic. With it they become powerful, capable of intimacy, self-disciplined, resilient, and compassionate. With mutual recognition, our children can become lions.

The concepts in this book are all designed to achieve the same thing: teach adults how to raise children who are psychologically strong and healthy. The Meet the Hand approach I propose develops a relationship between the adult and child that simultaneously creates the firm boundaries that builds connection and self-discipline while supporting the power and autonomy of the child that results in healthy self-expression and agency. When a "Meet the Hand" environment is created, it establishes a healthy psychological equilibrium. It holds things in balance and allows the development of power, connection, self-regulation and a real capacity for intimacy.

With average children, Meet the Hand will draw out and strengthen self-discipline, emotional regulation, independence and those characteristics that support respect for self and others. For children who have developed dysfunctional patterns of interaction and behavior, it can make the difference between suffering from characteristics that will be diagnosed "disordered" or "disabled" and bringing these characteristics back into a healthy range.

My goal is to shift the way we view children to one that looks more seriously at the role our interactions play in shaping the development of behavior, cognition and neurology. But that's not to say that a child-rearing approach that is based on mutual recognition should feel in any way contrived or stilted. On the contrary, parenting and teaching based on the principles of mutual recognition should allow both adults and children to build natural, healthy relationships based on their most authentic selves.

This style of authentic child rearing should feel deeply satisfying, but it will not be achieved without struggle and effort. We are perhaps the first generation of parents and teachers whose children's mental health depends on our taking up the gauntlet to evolve the way we raise them.

Our children are becoming lions and we must help them. We cannot do this by regressing and reverting to the authoritarian methods of the past. Nor can we turn our backs on traditional common sense, relinquishing our roles and responsibilities as adults. It is time to learn from the past and move forward in a new way.

For updates to this book, video tutorials and a schedule of Joe Newman's appearances go to RaisingLions.com

Glossary

Power – A child's ability to recognize and take initiative on their own wants, needs, interests and opinions. Power can be exerted aggressively as with yelling, crying or physical aggression, or by passive means such as feigning inability or lack of understanding in order to avoid some undesirable effort or consequence. Power stems from self-recognition. Texts on intersubjective theory refer to power as "agency."

Connection – A child's ability to respect the needs and desires of others, to have empathy for others and a capacity for close friendships as well as intimate relationships are all a result of ability for connection. Connection is the ability to recognize others as like you. Texts on inter-subjective theory refer to connection as "intimacy."

Mutual Recognition – The ability to have a healthy recognition of both yourself and others. This healthy tension between an ability to love yourself and respect and consider the needs of those around you develops the psychological muscles that manifest as self-regulation, self-discipline and a real feeling of connection to others. Mutual recognition can be said to form the most basic component of mental health.

Oneness – A child's first self-identity. At this stage a child doesn't see a separation between himself and his parents. Rather, his parents are perceived as an extension of his own person. Children begin to shift out of this perspective between the ages of eight and fourteen months.

Omnipotence – A child's second self-identity. In this stage the child recognizes and asserts his own power but has not yet recognized the power of others. Consequently, the child attempts to coerce adults into satisfying all his wants and alleviate all his frustrations.

Interdependence – In this stage the child no longer feels compelled to control those around him because he has come to realize he is both independent of others and dependent on them. This recognition of both his independent power and the power of others is the beginning of mutual recognition. In this state the child has learned to handle many of his difficulties and frustrations himself rather than insisting that adults handle them.

System of Interaction – The set of boundaries and interactions that determines whether a child remains within the omnipotent identity or transitions to the interdependent identity. A system that is capable of holding firm boundaries while recognizing and acknowledging the child's power will allow the development of healthy mutual recognition within the child. The System of Interaction can also be called a ***Holding Environment.***

Made in the USA
Lexington, KY
19 September 2016